TEARS TO JOY

TEARS TO JOY

ONE MAN'S JOURNEY
THROUGH GRIEF

MIKE TUCKER

Pacific Press®
Publishing Association
Nampa, Idaho | Oshawa, Ontario, Canada
www.pacificpress.com

Cover design by Steve Lanto
Cover design resources from iStockphoto.com / iStock-664692462, iStock-502665523
Inside design by Kristin Hansen-Mellish

Copyright © 2018 by Pacific Press® Publishing Association
Printed in the United States of America
All rights reserved

The author assumes full responsibility for the accuracy of all facts and quotations as cited in this book.

Unless otherwise noted, Scripture quotations are from the King James Version.

Scripture quotations marked NASB are taken from the NEW AMERICAN STANDARD BIBLE®, copyright © 1960, 1962, 1963, 1968, 1971, 1972, 1973, 1975, 1977, 1995 by the Lockman Foundation. Used by permission. www.lockman.org

Scripture quotations marked NKJV are taken from the New King James Version®. Copyright © 1982 by Thomas Nelson. Used by permission. All rights reserved.

Additional copies of this book are available for purchase by calling toll-free 1-800-765-6955 or by visiting http://www.adventistbookcenter.com.

Library of Congress Cataloging-in-Publication Data
Names: Tucker, Mike (Michael Duane), author.
Title: Tears to joy / Mike Tucker.
Description: Nampa : Pacific Press Publishing Association, 2018.
Identifiers: LCCN 2017053286 | ISBN 978-0-8163-6363-6 (pbk. : alk. paper)
Subjects: LCSH: Grief—Religious aspects—Christianity. |
  Bereavement—Religious aspects—Christianity. | Tucker, Mike (Michael
  Duane) | Tucker, Gayle Anne Whitacre Tucker, -2016.
Classification: LCC BV4909 .T84 2018 | DDC 248.8/66—dc23 LC record available at https://lccn.loc.gov/2017053286

January 2018

Dedication

Gayle and I were married for forty years, three months, thirteen days, and three hours before her death on April 10, 2016. Two of the very best things to come out of our marriage were our daughters, Allison and Michal. This book is dedicated to our daughters.

These two godly women remind me of their mother every day. Their passion for Jesus, love for others, dedication to our family, devotion to their church, and desire to see others in heaven are traits they learned in large part from their mother's example. Like Gayle, they are amazingly intelligent and well read, uncommonly excellent in their fields, and incredibly talented musically. And like Gayle, Allison and Michal reveal the love of Jesus to everyone around them every day of their lives.

Many families are torn asunder by a loss as significant as theirs. But these two women have been doggedly determined that our family will not experience that fate. They have instead forged an even deeper relationship with each other and with me through this terrible ordeal.

The summer after her mother's death, Allison changed careers, leaving her position as principal of a K–12 Christian school to become a pastor in the same church where her mother and I pastored for seventeen years. She carries some of the same responsibilities her mother held in that church and occupies the same office her mother used for all of her tenure there. Gayle knew about Allison's upcoming career change and was thrilled for her. I am brimming with pride at the fantastic job she does ministering to children, women, and seniors in that wonderful congregation.

Michal's marriage to Levi has grown stronger even though this sort of loss often has the opposite effect on marriages. Michal and Levi have labored with amazing skill and tenderness as they have helped their children grieve the loss of "Grammy" in a healthy manner. These two parents have not allowed Gayle's death to destroy their home. Instead, they have constantly amazed me with wisdom that surpasses their years. I stand in awe of them as parents and as a married couple. I also am in awe of the incredible skill Michal displays as a counselor who daily assists people in every facet of life.

While this book will focus mainly on my journey, it could just as easily focus on Allison's and Michal's journeys through sorrow. I owe much to both of them and truly doubt that my recovery would be what it is without their love and support.

Allison and Michal, the two of you are the crowning achievements of my life with your mother. We both have loved and cherished you. I look forward to the day we see your mother again. Gayle will not be surprised at the stories I tell her of how you dealt with her death. She will be thankful to learn that you have lived well and loved well.

Table of Contents

Preface	9
Introduction	11
Section 1: Loss	**13**
Chapter 1: The Experience of Loss	15
Chapter 2: Anticipation and Lazarus	21
Chapter 3: My Experience With Loss	24
Chapter 4: Your Experience With Loss	34
Section 2: Difficulties	**47**
Chapter 5: Adjustments	49
Chapter 6: Surprises	52
Chapter 7: Expectations and Criticisms	55
Chapter 8: Pace	61
Chapter 9: Guilt	63
Chapter 10: Awkwardness	66
Chapter 11: Loneliness and Community	68
Chapter 12: Crosswinds, Sorrow, and Joy	71
Chapter 13: Tears	74
Chapter 14: Good Days, Bad Days, and Hope	76
Chapter 15: Holidays and "Firsts"	78
Chapter 16: Character of God	83

Chapter 17: Anger With God—Part 1	87
Chapter 18: Anger With God—Part 2	89
Chapter 19: Anger With and/or Guilt About the Deceased	92
Chapter 20: Justifiable Anger	94
Chapter 21: Suicide	99
Chapter 22: Purging and Disloyalty	101
Chapter 23: Of Shrines and Hearts	104
Chapter 24: The Journey, Memories, and Progress	107
Chapter 25: Severe Mercies, Amazing Grace	110
Chapter 26: The One-Year Anniversary	112
Section 3: Helping Those in Grief	**115**
Chapter 27: Support	117
Chapter 28: Myths in Grief	120
Chapter 29: Vacations From Grief	122
Section 4: Moving On	**125**
Chapter 30: Joy in the Morning	127

Preface

For years in my work as a counselor, pastor, and chaplain, I have taught classes on grief recovery. I pointed to the research, talked about my own experience, and shared the stories of grief from those I had been able to help. All in all, my teaching was helpful, and many people acknowledged the value it brought to their own process of recovery.

Although I had experienced losses in my own life, I never had the life-altering, devastating loss that is only experienced through the death of a mate or a child or through divorce. These three losses are among the worst that humans experience in life.

All of that changed on April 10, 2016, when Gayle Anne Whitacre Tucker—my wife, best friend, and colaborer of more than forty years—passed away. Her loss was unlike anything I had ever experienced before.

My life was in shambles, but losing Gayle had another unexpected impact. Her death put to the test everything I had ever taught in every grief-recovery class through the decades. It forced me to reevaluate everything I taught and thought I knew.

After putting my own teaching to the test, I can tell you with full confidence that the published literature and the time-tested research is, in fact, reliable. While every person and every experience of loss is different, the literature still applies and can be of inestimable value.

I followed, to the best of my abilities, my own advice and found it to be worthy of the confidence I had previously placed in it. The things I had taught are true, the methods of dealing with the loss are useful, the philosophies are reliable, and recovery is indeed a possibility.

Tears to Joy

It is my goal to share with you some of what I have taught and experienced. In addition to what I have taught, I found a few new insights that have also been helpful. It is my fervent prayer that this material will be of value to you as you make your own journey through the losses of life.

Finally, I hope this book serves as a small tribute to Gayle. Her life had a positive impact on millions through seminars, television programs, and many years as a pastor and teacher. I pray that this book will in some small way serve to continue Gayle's ministry for years to come.

Special thanks are owed to Jennifer LaMountain, Casey Tom Baker, Pam Tucker, and Vicki Tucker for their encouragement, editorial assistance, inspiration, and suggestions that helped to improve this book. The time and talent you have contributed to this project have not gone unnoticed. Thank you for helping to make this book a reality.

Introduction

This book is the journal of one man's experience with loss. It makes no claims to be the be-all and end-all of grief books. My experience may differ widely from yours, and my road to recovery may not look exactly like yours. There will be, however, the inevitable similarities. It is in these areas of commonality that you will likely find the greatest help in dealing with your loss.

Included in the book is my personal story of loss and excerpts from blogs on my journey as well as articles from various publications that were either written by me or were written about my loss. Clinical information, suggested exercises, and stories will be shared to assist in facilitating recovery.

Death is not the only significant loss of life. Other losses occur with sexual assault, mastectomy, amputation, loss of a job, and many more instances. While this book will focus primarily on losses through death, the principles apply to other losses. The suggested exercises may be altered to fit different types of loss.

It is my deep hope that this book will help you even in the midst of your sorrow. If it does nothing more than encourage you to simply place one foot in front of the other, then I will count it a success.

Blessings to you as you learn to live on without your loved one(s). May you find courage for this, life's most difficult journey.

Section 1

Loss

What are the losses of life? What effect do they have on us physically, mentally, emotionally, and spiritually? Is there a better way to deal with our losses? If so, what is that way?

While there is no magic pill for recovery, I do believe there are things you can learn that will help you in your own journey to recovery. Join me as we begin the process of analyzing loss, its effect on us, and how we might better deal with it.

Chapter 1

The Experience of Loss

No one lives life without experiencing loss. Loss occurs with the death of a pet, friend, or relative; a divorce or the abandonment of a lover; the moving away of a friend or the moving out of a child; the failure to reach a goal, realize a dream, keep or obtain a job; the removal of a body part through amputation or mastectomy; and many other ways. While these losses may vary greatly in severity, each may require some experience of grief.

Grief could be described as the process of psychological, social, and spiritual reactions to loss. It involves intense emotional suffering, acute sorrow, and deep sadness. The mourner remembers the deceased, and this produces uncomfortable, anxious feelings and deep sadness. Symptoms of grief include but are not limited to the following:

- tightness in the throat or heaviness in the chest
- an empty feeling in the stomach often accompanied by a loss of appetite
- feelings of guilt or anger
- restlessness
- loss of concentration
- loss of interest in activities that you used to love
- short-term memory loss
- feeling as though the loss isn't real or that it didn't really happen
- sensing the loved one's presence, expecting the person to walk in the door at the usual time

- hearing the loved one's voice, or seeing his or her face
- having difficulty sleeping
- experiencing an intense preoccupation with the deceased
- feeling intensely angry at the loved one for leaving
- needing to tell and retell stories about the loved one
- experiencing frequent mood changes
- crying at unexpected times

As if all that were not enough, people in grief have immune systems that function at less than optimum, are at greater risk of infection and illness, and even have a greater likelihood of sudden death. Their energies are depleted, and they find themselves less able to deal emotionally and physically with the daily challenges life brings. Everything, no matter how seemingly small, is a big deal! Things that are normally easy now become difficult.

The most intense symptoms may last anywhere from six months to two years! Typically, most people report that the most intense symptoms dissipate at the six- to nine-month mark and then increase sharply at the one-year anniversary of the loss. Following the anniversary, they dissipate once again. But it is possible to grieve actively for up to four or five years without being obsessive with your grief. The rule of thumb is *the sooner and more intensely you grieve, the sooner you get better.*

The last sentence of the previous paragraph may be one of the most important things I can say in this book. Intense, early grieving has been a helpful concept for my own experience with loss. While my journey through grief may be quite different from yours, I firmly believe the concept of early, intense grief to be one of the most impactful ideas I can share.

On the other hand, the longer you delay grieving, the longer it takes to get through the process and the more difficult it becomes. You may be able to ignore grief for a time, but eventually it will catch up with you and exact from you a very dear price. Early, intense grief is a far better approach to any loss.

Once I met a man whose wife died suddenly. The man chose to avoid grief by working insanely long hours seven days a week. He did this for more than ten years! Then he met a woman, fell in love (when he found time to do this, I'll never know!), and asked her to marry him. As the two began to prepare for their wedding day, the man was reminded of his first wedding. That memory seemed to set loose a flood of emotions. The emotions, long suppressed, were now so intense and so overwhelming that the man required hospitalization.

The Experience of Loss

His wedding had to be postponed while he finally grieved the loss of his wife.

There is no way around grief. Loss necessitates it. You cannot run from grief, medicate it, ignore it, outwork it, outdrink it, or rationalize or spiritualize it away. You must go through it. If you attempt to ignore grief, it will eventually catch up with you. And when it does, it will take longer and be a more difficult process than it would have been had you grieved intensely and early.

Every loss requires some experience of grief. It is unavoidable. The experience for some losses may be light and of shorter duration while other losses result in a heavy experience of grief that may last for some time.

In some sense, one never truly recovers from a loss. While the symptoms of loss may dissipate or even leave completely, you will never truly get over your loss. You will forever be changed by your loss and may have periods of sorrow and tears for the rest of your life.

My sister and brother-in-law lost a baby early in their marriage. The baby died late in my sister's pregnancy. While my sister grieved over the loss, my brother-in-law didn't. More than twenty-five years later, while sitting in church at the funeral for a friend, my brother-in-law began weeping uncontrollably. As he processed his tears, he realized he was crying over the baby they had lost many years earlier; a loss he had never truly grieved.

My sister states that for five years after the loss of her baby, she would burst into tears for seemingly no reason. While sitting at a stoplight or shopping for groceries, sorrow would overwhelm her. It's been thirty years since she lost that baby, but from time to time she still feels the need to cry about her baby.

As difficult as the process of grief may be, *it is possible to deal with the pain in such a way that eventually you will once again find joy and a renewed purpose for life.* But this seldom occurs unless you do the hard work of grief.

The work of grief

What is the work of grief? Four activities come to mind: think, write, talk, and cry. These four activities are essential to the process. Let's look at each of these activities.

Think. Take a memory trip through the house or other areas that remind you of the lost person. For the bereaved, remembering is a sacred act! Relive many experiences in your mind. Think the thoughts fully when they come, whether the thoughts are pleasant or painful. Thinking and remembering are of vital importance.

Write. Keep a journal or notebook. Writing blog posts can be of real value as well. Write about your feelings. If you don't write, try making an audio or video recording about your feelings. Whether you write or make a recording, tell the story of the deceased's life and, more important, tell the story of your life together. How did you meet? What were the early years like? How did the relationship change through the years? What are some of the more significant, romantic, or even funny stories that are of importance to you?

For losses that do not involve the death of a loved one, it is still important to write about the meaning of that which was lost. For example, women may need to write about the impact of a mastectomy. This includes feelings of beauty and femininity as well as maternal feelings. The loss of a job can reach far beyond the expected financial and career implications for both men and women. The impact this loss has on self-esteem is huge. Writing about these things can be of real value.

Talk. Talk with dear friends, counselors, or even with a support group. Details should be told over and over, but you especially need to express your feelings. Talk about the immediate loss. Move back through your total relationship with the person. Express your deepest feelings. Tell your story, even if the story is not a happy story. Even the loss of a dysfunctional relationship must be grieved. These stories are as important to tell as are the stories from healthy relationships.

Cry. Don't hold back your tears. Tears are cleansing, so enjoy the therapeutic release provided by your tears.

These four activities compose the essential work of grieving. Others might add such things as exercise, a regular (although not too hectic) daily schedule, joining a support group, prayer, and more. But the activities you must engage in in order to do the work of grief are to think, write, talk, and cry.

My personal experience has found two of the above additional activities to be of real value. *Prayer* and regular, moderate *exercise* have been of inestimable help in my own personal journey. For exercise, I have chosen simply to walk. Since grief makes it next to impossible to focus for long periods of time, I have chosen to follow the advice given by D. L. Moody regarding prayer. Moody said that prayer should be frequent, brief, and intense. I have endeavored to follow this advice.

Adding these two elements to the more classic four activities of grief has been a real help in my recovery, and I recommend them to you.

Don't expect the journey of grief to be brief. Be gentle with yourself, and don't hold yourself to the expectations or timetables others may attempt to impose

The Experience of Loss

on you. This is *your* journey, to be made in *your* way, on *your* timetable. While it is also important that you not ignore experts in the field, you will be safe in doing things your way as long as your experience seems to fall within the "normal" range for healthy mourning.

Above all, try to do some of the work of grief every day. Think, write, talk, and cry daily. No doubt, you will take backward steps some days. This is to be expected and is quite normal. But don't lose patience with yourself or even with the process. You *will* get through this, but it may take some time.

Why grieve?

Grief actually has a purpose. We grieve in order to accomplish an objective. The objective is reorganization.

Grief serves as a tribute to the person we've lost. *We grieve greatly because we have loved greatly.* Grief's intensity (not necessarily its length) is directly related to the depth of love we held for the deceased. But it is easy to become so caught up in the tribute that we forget the objective.

I think of grief as a vehicle that takes us from point A to point B. Now admittedly, it's a rather sorry vehicle. It's an old, beat-up Edsel. (Anyone remember how ugly those cars were and how much America hated them?) This Edsel has more than three hundred thousand miles on it, is a gas-guzzler and oil burner, is in serious need of bodywork, and has a tire or two that frequently go flat. The grief Edsel doesn't do much more than thirty-five miles per hour on a good day, but it's the only ride we've got. *Grief* is the vehicle that takes us from the point of loss, which we will call "Disorganization," to the point of "Reorganization" and, hopefully, "Renewal."

Grief is the emotional suffering we experience when someone we love is taken away. It also involves physical, cognitive, social, behavioral, cultural, religious, and philosophical dimensions. It involves remembering, telling stories, longing, weeping, experiencing deep sorrow, and eventually adjusting to life without that person in it. As painful as it is to think of life without our beloved, it is nonetheless the objective of grief—the thing we've been moving toward all the time.

My own personal process of grief has been difficult, deep, and I believe, thorough. I've dealt with every memory that came to mind, both happy and sad, and I've been as intentional as I know how to be in accomplishing all the tasks and goals of grief. Now it is time to truly march toward the ultimate destination. It is time to begin in earnest my life without Gayle.

Tears to Joy

I would have preferred to grow old with Gayle, and one day, when I was ninety-five and she was ninety-two, we'd go to sleep and neither would wake up the following morning. Laugh if you will at that fantasy, but that's how I would have preferred it to happen. But I was not afforded that choice.

Since I am somewhat younger than ninety-five (no jokes here), I must assume I have a fair amount of living to do yet if God so allows. *Grief, as ugly as it is, is the only vehicle that is capable of transporting me from the tragedy of my loss to the reality of my future. I pray that future includes faith, ministry, family, hope, love, and joy.* Life is too short and too good when lived well to choose anything other than as full a life as we are capable of living. I want that life! My grief is making it possible for me to experience, yet again, life more abundantly. It can do the same for you!

Exercises

1. What are your symptoms? What do you feel? Are you sleeping? Eating? Crying? Easily distracted and have a tendency to forget things? Make a list of your symptoms today, and keep this list for future reference.
2. Begin writing something about your loss. You might start by writing about your symptoms and feelings as they are right now. Another idea is to begin to write the story of your life with the deceased. Start at the beginning. It doesn't have to be a literary work of art. Just let the words flow and see what happens.
3. Make a list of people you might begin talking to. It is best to have more than one person so that you don't wear anyone out. If a person wants to know what you want, simply say you need him or her to listen without judging, fixing, or evaluating your words; simply listen and pass you tissues when needed.

Chapter 2
Anticipation and Lazarus

Most people believe sudden, unexpected deaths to be among the most difficult to deal with. But long, protracted illnesses present their own unique set of difficulties.

Larry watched as his wife struggled with bone cancer for three years. During the final weeks of her life, Ruth endured unspeakable indignities and pain. It was a long, gruesome process for both Larry and Ruth to endure. When death finally drew near, the couple viewed it as a welcome relief.

During those awful months, Larry experienced something he hadn't expected. He found himself grieving for his wife while she was still alive. At first, he felt guilty, as though this premature experience of grief signaled that he was all too willing to give up and bring an end to his wife's suffering. He confessed such to me.

I shared with Larry that there was a name for the things he was experiencing. "Anticipatory grief," as it is called, is common in cases of long illnesses and can be healthy.

Anticipatory grief gives family members an opportunity to imagine the unimaginable. They begin to imagine life without their loved one. This process can aid in the adjustments that will need to be made when the death actually occurs.

Anticipatory grief also provides an opportunity for family members to remember their history with the loved one. Memories can be funny, happy, sad, pleasant, or unpleasant. Processing all of these memories can help place the relationship in perspective, demonstrating a purpose to the life of their loved one. Family members are also given an opportunity to say such things as, "I'm sorry," "I forgive you," or "I'm going to miss you." Goodbyes are always difficult, but taking the opportunity to do so before the loved one passes away can be helpful for everyone.

Those who engage in anticipatory grief may find a benefit to their grief experience when the loss ultimately occurs. For a few, the time required for grief may be shortened. Most will at least find that some of the highs and lows of grief will be made less dramatic and the adjustments a bit easier to accommodate.

My family was able to engage in some anticipatory grief after we received Gayle's diagnosis of stage 4 pancreatic cancer. That diagnosis is little more than a death sentence, and we knew it. Gayle was diagnosed just twenty-four days prior to her death. During those three and a half weeks, we were all forced to imagine life without Gayle.

Another phenomenon may often accompany a long illness. At times, the patient will be at the point of death only to rally suddenly and without explanation. Doctors and nurses may tell the family that death is imminent, and the family may gather around the bedside only to have their beloved sit up and eat breakfast the next morning!

This roller coaster of emotions has been called the "Lazarus syndrome." While this term was originally applied to patients who failed to respond to CPR (cardiopulmonary resuscitation) but suddenly came back to life, it has also been used with terminally ill patients who repeatedly seem to fail and then rally before finally succumbing to the effects of the disease. Family members who watch this phenomenon find themselves on an emotional roller coaster. At one point, they ready their hearts for the imminent death of their loved one, only to find themselves engaging in conversation with the very person they were certain would be gone. When this happens several times, the emotional toll exacted from family members is huge.

When death occurs either from a long-term illness or after experiencing the Lazarus syndrome, the immediate response of the bereaved might be a collective sigh of relief. They may even believe they may be spared the typical experience of grief when in reality the relief is usually short lived. The normal symptoms of grief were only slightly delayed.

If your experience included anticipatory grief, the Lazarus syndrome, or both, realize that such occurrences are not uncommon. If you feel guilty over your own anticipation of the loss or even over the sigh of relief you may have breathed immediately after the death of your loved one, please know that such feelings of guilt are misplaced. Don't complicate your mourning with unnecessary guilt. Grief is difficult enough as it is!

Exercises
1. Was anticipatory grief a part of your experience? If so, do you believe it was helpful for your long-term recovery? Why, or why not?
2. Did you go through the Lazarus syndrome? How difficult was that experience for you and your family? Did you find an immediate sense of relief at the death of your loved one? If so, have you felt guilty over that sense of relief?

Chapter 3

My Experience With Loss

Early on, after my wife died, I began to write blog posts that I shared on Facebook. These posts became therapeutic for me; but much to my surprise, they also provided a great deal of help to those who read each post. I will tell a part of the story of my experience with loss by sharing some of the blog posts along with some articles that were written about the death of my wife, Gayle Tucker.

Gayle and I were married on December 28, 1975, in Tulsa, Oklahoma. We met while in college, and early on in our relationship I knew I would marry Gayle. She seemed to sense the same thing. The romance grew quickly. We began to discuss marriage after having dated a little over two months! We just knew we were meant to be together.

Throughout our forty years of marriage, Gayle and I raised a family (two daughters) and shared the experience of ministry together. We were blessed to work side by side in pastoral ministry as well as in the television ministry of Faith For Today. We cohosted the award-winning television program *Lifestyle Magazine* and collaborated on a recurring series of programs called *Mad About Marriage*. The marriage programs gave birth to a seminar by the same name. During the last six years of her life, Gayle and I traveled the world as we conducted 121 Mad About Marriage seminars together.

Ours was an easy marriage. While we certainly had our adjustments and disagreements, overall our marriage had very little drama and very few relationship difficulties. It seemed we were well suited for life together.

During the last twenty-five years of Gayle's life, we were together almost constantly. We worked, played, studied, wrote books, planned, and presented seminars together. About 90 percent of my travel was done with Gayle. Our lives were intricately intertwined.

But then everything changed. Here is a post I placed on Facebook that outlined the events that led to Gayle's death.

On Thursday, March 3, 2016, Gayle's right hand went numb. She was unable to use it properly. It was irritating to her but later in the day the hand returned to normal so she assumed she had slept on it wrong.

Friday, March 4, we flew to Vancouver, BC. That morning the hand was numb again. I had to carry most of the baggage since her hand didn't work but we assumed it would get better just as it had the previous day. By the evening when we were eating a meal with local pastors and the hand hadn't improved, I suggested we go to a hospital. Gayle said she wanted to wait until we were back in Dallas. But I stayed close to her that evening in order to help cover what we assumed was a temporary disability. We spoke to the pastors after the meal as Gayle held the microphone in her left hand since the right was unusable.

Saturday, March 5, I spoke for a church service as Gayle sat in the congregation. She didn't feel right. Her hand still was not working properly. After the service we took the sack lunches the ladies of the church had made and drove to the rented hall where we would present our marriage seminar. Gayle still wasn't feeling well. This was strange for her since in over 40 years of marriage I could count the number of times she had been ill on one hand.

Gayle remained in the car while I coordinated with the local volunteers and staffers at the rented hall. Once the computer was set up, the remote working properly, and sound was checked, I went to the car to get Gayle. Her hand wouldn't work but she looked radiant as ever as we walked into the hall together.

We presented for three and a half hours that day. Gayle stood in high heels, beautiful as a vision, holding the microphone always in her left hand. Her presentation was off about a fourth of a beat that day but I was the only one who would notice that since this was our one hundred twenty-first presentation of this seminar together. After the seminar Gayle rested backstage as I greeted people and collected our computer and other materials. Again, she refused to go to the hospital until we got back to Dallas.

Tears to Joy

Sunday, March 6, we flew direct from Vancouver to Dallas. When we landed I turned to Gayle and said, "Which hospital do you want me to take you to because we are not going home." She indicated the hospital she wanted, I collected the bags and we drove to the hospital.

When I explained her symptoms to the nurse we were taken ahead of everyone else and Gayle was rushed in for a CAT Scan. The initial diagnosis was strokes. Ten days and two hospital stays later that diagnosis was changed to stage 4 pancreatic cancer that had already spread to the liver. This cancer can cause a condition known in layman's terms as "sticky blood" which had resulted in a blood clot in Gayle's thigh. As the clots broke off they went to the brain causing strokes.

Eventually we took Gayle home to spend her final days with family and as many friends as I felt she could handle. She was as loving, kind, gracious, and courageous as ever during those days. I cherished each one of them.

Eventually the disease process was completed and Gayle passed away. But the time we had with her at home was quality. Remembering those days is both painful and joyous. Watching her die was difficult but experiencing her love of God, family, friends and me, was priceless.

My daughters and I were absolutely devastated by Gayle's death. Gayle was the glue that held us all together. She was the core of our family, my true love, my partner in ministry, and my partner in life. The thought of living without her was unbearable.

The first weeks after her passing were painful in ways that defy description. I have no words to explain what it was like. I could scarcely get out of bed in the mornings, much less get on with the work of ministry. It seemed as though my life had ended when Gayle died.

Gayle and I had lived very public lives. We were pastors of a very large and highly visible church, and we headed up a ministry whose television program we cohosted; a program that more than four million viewers watch every week in the United States and that is viewed by an unknown number internationally. That means that Gayle's illness and death were very public as well.

Some of the public attention we received during this time was awkward, while some was even painful. But I also have to admit that the attention and the accolades paid to Gayle after her death were actually healing for me. It was important to me that Gayle's life accomplishments and her sacrificial service would be, in some way, acknowledged. Gayle would have hated the attention paid to her, but having people write about the wonderful woman Gayle had been was meaningful to me.

The following is an article that appeared in the publication *Adventist Review* on April 11, 2016, the day after Gayle's passing.

Gayle Tucker, Beloved Marriage Counselor on Faith For Today TV, Dead at 60
The prominent Adventist television personality dies after a brief struggle with pancreatic cancer.

Gayle Tucker, one of the Seventh-day Adventist Church's best-known female television personalities, and a pastor, author, and counselor credited with lighting a fire under thousands of marriages, died less than a month after learning that she had pancreatic cancer. She was 60.

Tucker, associate speaker of the Faith For Today television ministry and co-host of its popular flagship "Lifestyle Magazine" program, died on Sunday, April 10, at her home in Dallas, Texas.

"I'm sorry to announce that Gayle Tucker passed away late this afternoon," Mike Tucker, her husband of 40 years and the speaker and director of Faith For Today, wrote Sunday night on Facebook. "She was surrounded by family and died peacefully."

Tucker turned to social media to chronicle his wife's brief struggle with cancer and to underscore that their faith would remain strong no matter what happened.

He announced the discovery of the cancer on March 19.

"Two weeks ago Gayle began having strokes. She had zero stroke risk factors and yet she had strokes," he wrote in the Facebook post. "It took almost a week and a half of MRI's, CT scans and more before they figured it out. Gayle has pancreatic cancer that has spread to her liver. This cancer can cause strokes.

"While medicine has no cure for this condition, we know the Master Physician and trust Him," he said. "We will accept His will whatever it may be."

About a week later, Tucker said in a follow-up post that his wife was resting better and had gained some physical strength.

"Gayle's faith is strong, her courage high, and her hope secure," he said. Several times he thanked well-wishers for their overwhelming support through prayer, cards, letters, Facebook messages, and e-mails.

"We love you all so much!" he wrote on March 29. "Gayle weeps with every new story or testimony of love for her. In fact, we can't share all of them with her since it causes her to weep, her love for you is so great."

Daniel R. Jackson, president of the Adventist Church in North America and a friend of the Tuckers for the past decade, paid tribute to Gayle Tucker on Monday for having a tremendous impact on married couples and for modeling a remarkable commitment to ministry.

"Gayle was loyal to God, to Mike, to her family, and to the church, in that order," Jackson said in an e-mailed statement. "She was a gracious, mature Christian who was passionate to let people know that the gospel of Jesus could and should be played out in everyday life and in everyday relationships."

He and others noted that Gayle Tucker had a warm personality that sparked immediate friendships.

"My most memorable moment with Gayle was the first time I met with her and Mike," he said. "There was an almost instant connection with her and Mike that lasted until this day."

He was echoed by Elaine Oliver, co-director of the Adventist world church's Family Ministries department, who with her husband, Family Ministries co-director Willie Oliver, conducted marriage conferences with the Tuckers across North America from 2000 to 2010.

"The first time we presented together at our one-day marriage conference 'From This Day Forward,' I was battling nerves and stage fright," Elaine Oliver said. "Gayle held my hands and prayed for me, reminding me that God was going to give me the strength and courage I needed. Her gentle strength was so comforting and reassuring."

From Schoolteacher to TV Personality

Gayle Ann Whitacre was born Aug. 26, 1955, in Tulsa, Oklahoma, to Jack and Ethel Whitacre, the owners of a small glass business.

Gayle, the second oldest, attended Adventist schools through college, graduating in 1976 with an elementary education degree from Southwestern Adventist College (now Southwestern Adventist University) in Keene, Texas.

It was at Southwestern that she met Mike Tucker, and the two were married on Dec. 28, 1975 in Tulsa.

My Experience With Loss

After teaching school for several years, Tucker joined her husband in full-time ministry at the 2,000-member Arlington Seventh-day Adventist Church in Arlington, Texas, where Mike Tucker served as senior pastor. She worked at the church as an associate pastor for 16 years, serving as the pastor of administration, music, and worship, with a special focus on children's and women's ministries. She was the first woman to become a credentialed commissioned minister in the Adventist Church's Southwestern Union Conference, which includes Texas.

In 2004, Mike Tucker took the helm at Faith For Today, the oldest religious television broadcast in the world, and his wife joined him on the team. She later became co-host of "Lifestyle Magazine" in 2007 and associate speaker in 2009.

"I believe Gayle Tucker was the most recognized Adventist female television personality in our denomination," Gordon Pifher, president of the North American Division's Adventist Media Ministries and chair of the Faith For Today executive committee, said in a statement. "Gayle had millions of fans and followers as host and co-host of the award-winning 'Lifestyle Magazine' program."

Faith For Today and "Lifestyle Magazine," which airs on more than 150 television channels worldwide, will continue to broadcast, Pifher said.

"But Gayle will be greatly missed," he said.

William Fagal, whose parents, William A. and Virginia Fagal, founded Faith For Today in 1950, recalled having several conversations with Gayle Tucker, including one at the Faith For Today booth at the General Conference Session in San Antonio last July.

"Gayle was radiant, full of life, and passionate about God's work," said Fagal, who retired as associate director of the Ellen G. White Estate last year. "Her loss leaves a large hole, not only in the lives of those who knew and loved her, but in the ranks of God's church."

Tucker used her background in elementary education to make family relationships a key focus of her ministry. She and her husband co-created "Mad About Marriage," a seminar project that includes a television series, marriage seminars, and small group curriculums; and co-authored the books *Mad About Marriage*, *Mantras for Marriage*, and *Marriage Moments*.

Willie Oliver said he would long remember listening to Gayle Tucker pray ahead of the marriage seminars that he and his wife presented with the Tuckers for 10 years. At the time, Willie and Elaine Oliver directed Family Ministries for the North American Division.

"My most memorable moment about Gayle was listening to her prayers on behalf of our own families and the couples we would be ministering to the following day," Willie Oliver said. "Her words, tone of voice, and deep faith in God always moved me to greater trust in the mission God had given us to accomplish together on behalf of His children."

Model of a Godly Woman
Funeral services for Gayle Tucker will be held at 3 p.m. April 16 at the Arlington Seventh-day Adventist Church.

She is survived by her husband, Mike; two adult daughters, Allison Tucker and Michal Anne Whitcomb; son-in-law Levi Whitcomb; and two grandchildren. Preceded in death by her father, she is also survived by her mother, Ethel Whitacre; sisters Joni Darmody and Julie Little; brother Jackson Whitacre; adopted brother Jon Whitacre; and two nieces and seven nephews.

Family and friends described Gayle Tucker as a living example of a godly woman.

"There are a few women who stand out to me as virtuous women—as the embodiment of Christ. And without a doubt I saw that inner beauty in Gayle the first time I met her," said Jennifer LaMountain, development director at Faith For Today, a singer, and a member of [the] Tuckers' extended family.

"She was a pastor at the time and I had come to provide a concert at her church," she said. "What a relief it was to meet Gayle and realize she had already thought through every need, every situation, and had everything in hand. . . . Calmly, joyfully, and easily she navigated everything required for creating an environment of true worship."

Steve Darmody, Tucker's brother-in-law and a friend for more than 40 years, said the words of Micah 6:8—"do justice, love kindness, and walk humbly with God"—were a fitting description of his sister-in-law's life.

"There are no better words to describe how Gayle Ann Whitacre Tucker actually lived her life," said Darmody, a gospel recording artist and president of the Morning Song Music Group. "Gayle fulfilled this biblical mandate with body, heart, mind, and spirit."

My Experience With Loss

Elaine Oliver said another passage of the Bible came to mind when she thought about Gayle Tucker.

"She epitomized the woman in Proverbs 31. She was a strong woman of faith who adored her husband, doted on her children and grandchildren, and was a fierce protector of her family," Oliver said. "I'm a better wife, mother, and ministry leader because of what I've learned from Gayle."

Gayle's life was spent in ministry to others. Her love for Jesus, people, her family, and me is a part of what made her so special. While nothing could replace the value she brought to my life, realizing that her life truly mattered was especially valuable to me.

Remembrances

One of the concerns experienced by those of us who grieve for a loved one is that the person we love so dearly will be forgotten. We fear that our loved one's contributions to the world will not be remembered. And if our loved one is forgotten, it almost feels as though his or her life was somehow wasted or perhaps didn't matter. It may also suggest to us that in some way we feel as though our own lives were wasted if we forget the loved one we've lost. In our more sane moments, we realize this is not the case; but as time passes and fewer people speak of our loved one, we are almost panicked at the thought that one so special could be so soon forgotten.

While living in the public eye certainly has its drawbacks, it also brings with it a few bonuses. The current bonus is the fact that so many people continue to remember Gayle, her talents, her love, and her contributions.

The bonus of remembrances began with her funeral. The church where the funeral was held is supposed to hold about six to seven hundred people, but more than eleven hundred attended Gayle's service with another four hundred watching by closed-circuit TV at a nearby school and another two to three thousand watching online. Not long after the funeral, posthumous awards started to come. Gayle and I were awarded a Lifetime Achievement Award in Family Ministries by the General Conference of Seventh-day Adventists and a Lifetime Achievement Award for Excellence in Broadcasting by the North American Division of Seventh-day Adventists. The church where Gayle and I spent seventeen years of our ministry is building a new children's and youth complex that they have voted to name after Gayle.

Tears to Joy

As I travel around the world to speak, I am almost overwhelmed by people who offer condolences and then share with me what Gayle meant to them. Many of them never met Gayle but were influenced nonetheless by her work on television or the seminars we presented together. I've had women tell me that they attempted to model their life after Gayle's life and demeanor, even though they never had the privilege of meeting her in person.

For the entire year after Gayle's death, I continued to be amazed by the number of Facebook comments, email messages, Twitter responses, website contacts, and letters regarding the impact of Gayle's life and ministry. It was very gratifying to me and to our family.

As I remember Gayle and the tremendous impact of her life, I am reminded that many, many more have made significant contributions but have labored in near obscurity. Their lives and ministries are no less valuable or significant than Gayle's, and yet it feels to their loved ones as though no one remembers or cares.

I was blessed to receive so many reassurances that my wife's life will not soon be forgotten. That is a benefit of our very public lives. But for those of you grieving loved ones whose lives were equally significant yet without the public recognition afforded Gayle, please understand that Heaven recognizes the contributions made and celebrates them. Heaven will never forget! For God, remembering is a sacred act!

If you would like to help someone you know who is grieving the loss of a loved one, please offer to that person a remembrance of the deceased. Tell the grieving person a story of significance to you, or share the impact that individual made on your life. Offering such a remembrance will help reassure the mourning family that their loved one is not forgotten. It will remind us all that every life matters and every life is of great significance.

As time passes since Gayle's death, I am remembering others who have made significant contributions to my life, people such as Wayne Thurber, Elden Walter, George Akers, Ben Leach, Jack Whitacre, Fred Thomas, and many more who have helped make me the man I am today. I thank God for their lives and offer a small remembrance of each.

Their lives mattered! Every life matters! None are forgotten. Heaven marks each life, celebrates each life, and one day will make public every private, seemingly obscure act of love ever offered on this planet. No one is forgotten in heaven!

Exercises

1. Make a list of your symptoms today. Has there been any change from the last time you thought about your symptoms?
2. Continue to write the story of your life with the person you've lost. Fill in some details, and especially focus on the feelings you are having as you write this story.
3. Have you made a list of the people you would like to talk with? If so, now may be a good time to contact one of these people to request an appointment. Keep it short—thirty minutes to an hour—and use the time to tell your story and your memories and to share your feelings.
4. How would you like your loved one to be remembered? Is it important to you that this person not be forgotten? Does it help when someone mentions your loved one or shares a story about him or her?
5. Consider making a record of the life of your loved one. Some ways to consider would be to put together a scrapbook, write the story of the person's life, or create a Facebook page that is dedicated to your loved one.

Chapter 4

Your Experience With Loss

Your story is unique. Your experience with the person you've lost is also unique. Others in your family or among your close friends may have had a relationship with this person, but their relationship is not the same as yours. You had a relationship that was unlike anyone else's.

This means that your experience of grief will be unlike anyone else's. The time it takes you to grieve, the symptoms you experience, and the things you find to be helpful will be different for you than for others who are grieving the same person. That's because your personalities, experiences, and resources are different. It's also because their relationship with the person who died is different from yours. All of these factors and more make your grief experience unique to you.

I can also tell you that even though others have had significant losses in their lives, nobody—and I mean absolutely nobody—knows exactly how you feel. There may be similarities in their loss and yours, but *your loss is totally unique to you.*

That also means that while others may think they know what is right for you and may have a lot of advice, they don't know exactly what they would do were they in your shoes. It is impossible to know until you are the person experiencing it.

For decades, I have helped people deal with the loss of a spouse. I thought I might have a fairly good idea of just how devastating that loss is. I must tell you that I was wrong! I had absolutely no clue as to just how horrific the loss of a spouse truly was! Nobody knows unless they've experienced it.

The same is true for losses by divorce, the loss of a child, or any other significant loss. Unless you've been through it, you cannot possibly know. Nor can you predict how you will handle such a loss. You have to go through it in order to know.

There are some things most grievers have in common. For nearly every person experiencing grief, the pain is unbelievably strong. It is almost impossible to explain this feeling to someone who has never known heavy grief. It affects your sleep, appetite, memory, attitudes, likes and dislikes, and every other area of life. It makes you wonder whether you can live through the experience, and it may even make you wonder whether you actually want to live through it all.

When the experience of mourning is heavy, it seems as though it will never end. The truth is that things truly are changing, but the changes are so slight and so slow that life feels as though you've been stuck forever. This feeling is normal. Changes occur slowly, almost imperceptibly, for those in grief.

In order to keep some measure of perspective, many people find it helpful to keep a log of their symptoms. As you chronicle your feelings, sleep patterns, appetite, moods, and more, you can check back over the past few days or weeks and see that there actually has been change. Seeing evidence of even slow, small changes can be encouraging.

Overall, grief can victimize you. It can leave you with the feeling that you have absolutely no control. I can't stand that feeling. So I felt it was important to exercise at least some measure of control. The only way for me to do that was to have a plan. Having a plan helps restore a sense of control, even if you are not able to follow your plan in every detail. The plan combats the overwhelming sense of uncertainty that accompanies significant losses. Life itself seems fragile and tenuous. Having a plan tends to help alleviate those feelings.

The following are posts I shared on Facebook that outline my overall plan. Your plan may differ from mine. Your plan should fit your personality and your circumstances. No plan will be perfect, and no one ever sticks to the plan 100 percent of the time. But having and working a plan gives you at least a feeling of some measure of control, and that is extremely important.

Here is my plan.

The plan

When Gayle became ill, the staff at Faith For Today canceled all my appointments for the next three months. Gayle died a month after they had canceled everything, leaving me with two empty months. This proved to be both a blessing and a curse: a curse because I was alone in the house where

Tears to Joy

Gayle died with little to do, and a blessing because beside granting me time to do many of the things that are necessary after someone dies (hospital bills, insurance, death certificates, etc.), it also gave me an opportunity to plan how I would handle my loss.

Most people are unfamiliar with the symptoms and processes of grief. A lack of knowledge leaves many feeling at a loss to know how to make a plan. But I taught grief recovery for many years, so I was well acquainted with the literature and the research. I knew that people who have some sort of plan going in and who are able to work that plan are more likely to have a better experience than those who simply allow the waves of grief to toss them wherever it will. Thus, I created a plan.

I determined that I would grieve intensely and early. That was the *last* thing I wanted to do, but it was the *right* thing to do. I took my free time during those first two months to experience all of the pain and to begin the hard work of grief.

My plan was to engage with a vengeance in the four activities of grief: think, write, talk, and cry. I would add to those a few of my own: regular, moderate exercise (in my case, walking), prayer, and a determination to lean into the grief by anticipating painful experiences or events and engaging in those things sooner than would normally be necessary. I did not want to be "victimized" by grief any more than was absolutely necessary. So I decided to go on the offense rather than to passively wait and then react. To that end, I started speaking for camp meetings not quite two months after Gayle's death, did a Mad About Marriage seminar by myself, took a trip to New York City to do some of the fun things we used to do together, and even went on a cruise by myself just to ensure that I could do it.

It was important in my plan that I would be able to hold a positive view of God that hopefully would prevent me from blaming God for the loss and would instead help me thank Him for the gift of Gayle for more than forty years of my life. This view of God would enable me to realize that I have received far more than God has ever promised. I have been blessed with an embarrassment of riches in that I have had a love and partnership that few ever realize.

I made and followed plans for birthdays, major holidays, and family gatherings. And I kept in open and honest communication with people I knew would listen with empathy and without judgment.

I also promised myself that any major decisions would be made only after consultation with people whose opinion I trusted, and then I would follow their advice.

Because of the plan to meet grief head on, my experience over the first year was monumentally painful. I cried more than I thought humanly possible as I thought about Gayle daily and at times hourly. Confusion, an inability to focus, sadness, somatic disturbances, loss of appetite followed by comfort eating, mood swings, and more had all been a part of my daily existence. I was the textbook griever.

But I can honestly say that I remained faithful to my plan. Any "hiccups" were quite minor and unintentional. I didn't do any of the monumentally destructive things a great many people tend to do when caught in the throes of grief. I followed the plan, dealt with emotions, and conducted the entire process quite publicly in order to hold myself accountable—hoping to be of some value to someone with a similar loss.

As of this writing, I can say that I've slowly grown accustomed to my new normal. That the loss is undeniable has become my new reality. I have embraced the pain and I have made adjustments; a new identity is beginning to emerge; and hope has started to return. Gradually, my pain has eased. I've gotten used to the absence of my life partner and have moved toward the possibility of a new investment in life.

The plan has worked about as well as was realistic for me to hope it would. By God's grace, I've remained true to my values, principles, goals, and dreams. I've continued to minster and to live as I believe I should. It has not been easy, but God has given me strength just when I've needed it, making me more of a whole person again. He has also allowed me to gain a broader perspective on grief's journey.

The journey of grief has mile markers. As you pass the mile markers, you realize you are making progress. Skip over a marker, and you will pay for it.

Mile marker 1: Believe it really happened. You can't grieve a loss you don't believe you've actually had. Accepting the finality of the loss can be a difficult thing. As much as you'd like to deny it, your loved one isn't coming back until the resurrection.

Everyone has at least some difficulty with this. A few find the struggle to be very difficult. Accepting the reality of the loved one's absence is almost too painful to accept.

For me, this process was more of a natural, even unavoidable, process. When I woke up in the morning, I'd look next to me in my bed in order to truly believe that Gayle was gone. There were times when I wanted to call her to tell her something, but then it dawned on me that I couldn't do that. She was gone.

The sooner you come to grips with the reality of the loss and the sooner you enter in to the process of grief, the sooner you get better. But it all begins with accepting the loss.

Mile marker 2: Be willing to experience the pain. Some people try to hide from the pain. Others attempt to medicate themselves or numb themselves with alcohol. Other methods include work, pornography, a new love interest, or simply attempting to ignore the pain.

I chose to lean into the pain. I intentionally thought about Gayle, engaged in activities we used to do together, went places we used to go, and more. As much as it hurt, I embraced the pain, cried, thought the thoughts fully, and felt the depths of my sorrow. There were times when I thought I might be overwhelmed, but eventually it all hurt a bit less. For me, the most noticeable relief came about nine or ten months after Gayle's death. But that will vary greatly from person to person.

Mile marker 3: Make adjustments to daily life without that person in it. This, to some degree, is unavoidable. I had to learn to sleep, cook, take care of the house, and go to parties, and more by myself. Every aspect of life must be adjusted. Work, play, worship, and everyday mundane functions must all be adjusted. Even my self-concept, attitudes, and personal identity needed to be adjusted. Once I made a great many adjustments, I eventually began to identify a new normal. I didn't actually like my new normal—few do—but it is my unavoidable reality.

Some people are actually relieved to find a new normal. This may occur when they have had to care for their loved one for a very long time. Some people are very ill for years before they die. Once the death occurs, the caregiver may find an initial relief. This is normal. Any guilt associated with this sense of relief is misplaced.

Others may feel relief if the person they are grieving was extremely dysfunctional, mentally ill, or abusive. Any new normal could be an improvement! Again, this is normal. It is also normal to feel guilty over the sense of relief. Such guilt is misplaced but completely normal.

Mile marker 4: Say goodbye to the relationship, withdraw the emotional energy invested in that relationship, and reinvest. This one hurts, and few like doing it. But eventually there comes a time when you hate grieving so badly that you are willing to do it.

You don't say goodbye to your memories or your love for that person. You say goodbye to the relationship as it used to be and embrace the new relationship in your heart and mind. I must say goodbye to Gayle as my best friend, coworker, cook, and more. I may not do it all at once but gradually and bit by bit. As I do, I withdraw that emotional energy and reinvest. The thing I choose to reinvest in at first may change in a few weeks, months, or years. Usually the best investments are made in God and people. These are the most fulfilling too.

In many ways, I'm passing the fourth mile marker. This process may take longer for some and less time for others, but it must ultimately be passed. It is important that you don't try to rush to this marker. You must pass all the other markers before reaching the last mile marker. Pass it when you are ready and not before.

This fourth mile marker is the most difficult and the one about which I get the most questions. I'll do my best to unpack it a bit.

The fact is the relationship has changed significantly. The old relationship is gone and is irretrievable this side of heaven. The old relationship involved face-to-face communication, touch, sharing of memories, teamwork, and much more. The new relationship exists in your heart and your memories.

In essence, the old relationship has died. To acknowledge its passing, to say goodbye to it, to withdraw the emotional energy invested in that relationship, and to then reinvest is a healthy way to view that which has already taken place.

As much as I would love to, I cannot embrace Gayle or talk to her or share a memory with her. I remember going through family photos in an attempt to consolidate and reduce clutter. As I did, I found many photos of Gayle and our young family. I longed to talk to her and share those memories, but obviously, I could not.

The old relationship has died. The new relationship with Gayle lives on as long as I live, in my heart and mind.

Saying goodbye

Years ago I taught a six-week grief-recovery class for a hospital where I served as chaplain. The classes became popular, and we had large crowds for them.

At one of these classes, I remember seeing a woman in her late thirties. She attended every week and was very emotional through the sessions. But there were so many people in attendance that I was unable to visit with her in order to learn her story.

The next three times we held the class, this same woman was back but attended with a different person each time. I was unable to talk to her because of the size of the class.

About the fourth time this happened, I made a point of talking to the woman and was able to get her story. I was amazed by what she told me.

This woman had three sons. The youngest, a four-year-old boy, was truly "mama's boy." The older two were closer to their father, but the youngest son truly adored his mother. He was her constant companion and did everything with her.

One of the things he loved to do was to help her make banana muffins. When it was time to make them, the boy sat on the counter and helped his mother. He particularly loved to crack the eggs and put them in the mix, something he was exceptionally good at doing. He never got shells in with the eggs.

One day this woman was ready to make banana muffins and looked for her son. He was outside playing with his brothers and appeared to be having so much fun that she decided to make the muffins without him. When he came inside and discovered that the muffins had been made without him, he was upset. His mother promised that the next time she made them they would do so together.

It was soon after this incident that an accident happened, taking the boy's life. As you might imagine, this woman's grief knew no limits. She struggled with everyday life. Just getting out of bed was a monumental undertaking. Finally, at the insistence of her physician, she attended the grief-recovery class I was teaching.

She did pretty well until I mentioned the fourth goal of grief, to say goodbye to the relationship as it had existed, withdraw the emotional energy invested there, and reinvest it. The mere suggestion of this step made her angry! She vowed never to do this.

The woman's struggle with sorrow grew worse and worse. Finally one evening when she was unable to sleep, she got out of bed and wandered into the kitchen. She saw the bananas were not looking too good. Since she couldn't sleep anyway, she began to make muffins out of them.

It wasn't until she started to crack the eggs that she remembered the promise she had made to her son before his death. She broke down in tears, weeping uncontrollably.

Finally when she began to regain her composure, she decided to do the unthinkable. She said something like this: "Johnny, I love you more than I can say, but on this earth I will never again make banana muffins with you. So I must say goodbye to you as my banana muffin–making partner. I love you darling. Goodbye."

Once again the tears flowed; but as she looked back on that night, she realized that she had finally turned a corner. It was from that point that she began to improve.

Whenever someone in her neighborhood, church, or workplace experiences a loss, she now waits until things settle down for this person. Then when she thinks the time is right, she makes banana muffins, gives them to the bereaved person, and says, "These are banana muffins, and there is a story associated with them. When you're ready, I'll tell you the story."

She returns later at the appropriate time and tells the person the story. Then she takes that person with her to attend grief-recovery classes.

This woman took a horrendous loss and turned it into a grace for others. She withdrew the emotional energy she had invested with her son and reinvested it in service for others in the throes of grief. In addition to helping others, she also helped herself in her own recovery.

Moving on

As you pass this marker, your grief doesn't end. It never really ends, but it can become more manageable. *You can breathe more deeply, concentrate a bit more, make plans, and have hope for the future.* Your heart finds a bit more space to love, dream, hope, and simply live.

All of this happens differently for everyone. Some will take longer than others. Some move in starts and stops, while others move slowly and inexorably forward. It doesn't really matter how it happens for you because we are all different. What matters is that it happens. The process must, in one manner or another, move forward.

Life awaits. Not freedom from grief nor freedom from pain, but life. It is a life with memories both good and painful. It's a life with sorrow, joy, fear, elation, despair, and hope. But in the end it's still a life. It can be a life with meaning, purpose, and even joy. It's what we have. We must embrace the gift that remains.

This is my plan. It has worked as well for me as I could have hoped. Again, your plan may differ from mine, but hopefully you will find some elements of my plan that will prove to be of some value to you as you chart your course through the journey of grief.

Tears to Joy

Early in my experience of grief, I wrote an article for publication in the *Adventist Review*. The article appeared on April 23, 2016, just thirteen days after Gayle's death. It chronicles my initial experience with grief and demonstrates my attempts to follow my plan:

Coping With the Most Difficult Loss of My Life
Jesus remains my constant companion, my primary means of support.
By Mike Tucker, speaker and director, Faith For Today

Loss and the accompanying grief are inescapable parts of life. Everyone has experienced a loss of some sort, and everyone has had to deal with grief.

Like you, I've had many losses through the course of my life, but this most recent loss is by far the most crippling. For most, the loss of a spouse is among the most difficult. Though my loss is fresh and my journey through grief only just beginning, thus far this is the most difficult experience of my life.

Gayle was my soulmate. Gayle and I believed that soulmates are "created" rather than "found." Two people become soulmates when they decide to do whatever it takes to become soulmates. Gayle and I made that decision, did the work and, by God's grace, became closer than we could have ever dreamed. While this relationship made my life unspeakably rich, it has multiplied my loss with Gayle's passing on April 10.

We had 40 years of life, love, family and ministry! While we certainly have had our ups and downs as a couple, in the end we could say we've truly enjoyed the ride. When Gayle knew she was dying, she spoke to me of our marriage with the simple words, "No regrets!" I concur. Absolutely no regrets!

Gayle was my best friend. I miss telling her stories from my day, seeing her smile when our children and grandchildren come to visit, hearing her laughter, and feeling the warmth of her embrace. And I miss her prayers. I may miss her prayers most of all.

We studied Scripture together, discussed theology, planned and executed ministry initiatives, and played with grandchildren as a team. I can never replace those things.

Faith Amid Loneliness and Tears
I am a counselor and have worked as a hospice and hospital chaplain. In

those capacities I have taught many classes in grief recovery and counseled with many who are engaged in deep grief. In these professional capacities I have learned that it is sometimes helpful to let people know that their symptoms, while severe, are nonetheless normal. With that in mind I will share a few of my grief-related symptoms.

Loneliness can almost overwhelm me at times. I am fortunate to have a strong support system so this loneliness is not the absence of people in my life but the absence of my life mate. I miss her terribly!

Unlike many others who experience such a loss, I have not had a loss of faith. A temporary loss of faith is a frequent symptom of grief and is viewed as being quite normal and not necessarily a sign of spiritual weakness. With past losses I experienced this loss of faith, but that has not happened thus far in this current journey. Jesus remains my constant companion, my primary means of support. The hope of the Resurrection keeps me going from day to day.

I cry frequently, often at unexpected times. When I cry I make sounds that surprise me. They come from some place deep within and sound to me to be almost not human. These sounds are the most basic, and perhaps even the most eloquent, expressions of my pain.

Thus far I am sleeping five to seven hours a night. This is a blessing to me and is unusual for most in deep grief. My appetite comes and goes. My powers of concentration and memory are almost nonexistent, and I have lost interest in many of the things I used to enjoy. Gayle is the first thing on my mind every morning and the last thing on my mind every night. I am consumed by my memories and thoughts of my wife.

At times I feel a heavy weight pushing down on my shoulders and chest. I sigh frequently and seem to constantly have a lump in my throat as though I am always on the verge of tears.

All of this is normal.

Finding Strength in Prayer and Exercise
I have found a few things to be helpful thus far in my journey of grief. While these things do not "fix" my grief, they have helped me hold up under its burden.

Prayer is important to me. I am unable to pray for long periods of time and am often unable to kneel in prayer. Instead I pray as I walk, as I work, and as I move about the house or through an airport. My prayers are more brief conversations than formal petitions. Dwight L. Moody, the 19th-century U.S. evangelist, said that prayer should be brief, frequent, and intense. I agree and find this sort of prayer helpful in my journey.

It is more important than ever to focus on the positive elements of God's character. I find these to be most beautifully illustrated in the life of Christ. My reading comes from the gospels and takes place in short passages. When I read outside the Bible, I make certain it is light, positive, and inspiring. I focus on things that illustrate the love of God. Prophecy, end-time events, and deep theology are not helpful to me just now. Jesus is my all in all!

It is essential that I maintain a regular schedule. I have tried to limit my schedule so as to avoid overtaxing myself. I get out of bed about the same time every morning. (This often takes great effort.) Keeping a routine is important.

Diet and exercise are vital. Often when I have an appetite I crave junk. Instead, I try to focus on fruits and vegetables while avoiding my beloved enchiladas. (OK, I eat them from time to time, but not nearly as often as I crave them.)

And I walk. At my age, walking is a wonderful exercise. It gives me time to think and to pray. I begin with a morning walk of 4 ½ to 5 miles (7 to 8 kilometers). Then I make sure I walk during the day. The bank, grocery store, pharmacy, dry cleaners, and restaurants are all within walking distance from where I live. I leave the car in the garage and walk whenever possible. My record distance is 11.6 miles (18.6 kilometers) in one day. Eight to 10 miles (13 to 16 kilometers) is not uncommon. I joke that I am a "grief walker." I am literally walking my way through grief! I highly recommend it.

I have to force myself to engage socially. However, it is important to make the effort. While it is often difficult, social interaction with family and friends can be healing.

While these things are helpful, nothing truly stops the pain. There is no way to avoid grief. It must be experienced. You cannot go around it. You must walk through "the valley of the shadow of death." There is no escaping it.

However, I am finding that Jesus is not just walking with me, but that He is actually carrying me. Even when it feels as though He is far from me, He carries me.

I trust Him now more than ever and believe His promise that one day soon I will see Gayle again.

Until that day!

This article chronicles my attempts to grieve intensely and early. I fully believe this has been a major key to my adjustment to the loss. I established a plan, attempted to follow the plan, and gave myself to the process of grief immediately after the loss. This is my recommendation to you as well.

Exercises

1. Continue to log your symptoms. Note any changes that may have occurred from the last time you thought about your symptoms.
2. Continue to write the story of your life with the person you've lost. Fill in some details, and focus especially on the feelings you are having as you write this story.
3. Continue to talk to friends, pastors, or counselors who are committed to listening and lending their support.
4. Begin to create an outline of your plan. How will you chart your course through the process of grief? Write down your ideas. It's OK to edit the plan as you progress.

Section 2
Difficulties

Knowing what the journey may look like and knowing what activities you need to engage with in order to make the journey do not mean the trek will be without difficulties. *The road through grief is rough and winding. There are usually more switchbacks than straightaways.* It seems as though the entire journey is uphill on a fairly steep grade. This may be the most difficult journey you will ever take.

Everyone's path through grief is different, and a part of the difference comes from people who do not fully understand the journey. Their expectations, interference, and at times even their well-intentioned attempts at "helping" you may make the journey even more difficult.

Someone may say to you, "It's been six months. Aren't you over this yet?" Someone else may say, "It's only been fifteen months. Why do you think you can move on with your life?" Neither comment is helpful, nor do they demonstrate an understanding of the journey.

Even if your family and friends are all truly helpful, if you are like me, you will find plenty of ways to make the trip more difficult than it needs to be. I don't need outside help to make my journey arduous. I seem to be able to accomplish that all on my own.

The following chapters deal with some of the difficulties those in grief tend to face. Some of these troubles are created by the people in our lives, while others are self-inflicted.

Chapter 5
Adjustments

After the loss of a loved one, there are adjustments to be made. In fact, when listing the "goals" of grief, making adjustments to daily life without the person you've lost is the third goal on the list. Yet the adjustments continue throughout and even well beyond the process of grief. They don't happen all at once but take place simultaneously with the other three goals.

An adjustment can be something as simple as remembering to take out the trash because the person you lost was the one who always did it. Adapting to sleeping alone, cooking for one—or actually learning *how* to cook—having no one with whom to share your stories, or figuring out how to manage the finances are all examples of the many adjustments that must be made.

For me, the work adjustments were huge. Gayle and I planned together, wrote together, traveled and presented together, and cohosted television programs together. Gayle handled a myriad of details with dignity and grace and was wise enough to gently help me see the hidden difficulties that lay in store for my "creatively big ideas" without destroying my enthusiasm.

On the few occasions when I traveled without Gayle, I would call and share with her the stories of my day, the victories God had granted, and the challenges that lay ahead. She was always the first person I thought of when I had something to share. She was my best friend.

Family gatherings were organized and often hosted by Gayle. She would clean, cook, invite, decorate, welcome each guest, and make everyone feel right at home. She was the heart and soul of our family.

I suppose it is unrealistic to believe that every needed adjustment to the loss of a forty-year marriage could be made in a few months. While these challenges began immediately after her death, they continue to this day with no end in sight.

Yet with each new adjustment, I realize I am creeping ever so slowly toward life without Gayle. And while it is profoundly sad to even write the words *life without Gayle*, it is absolutely necessary that I continue to make that journey.

I try not to imagine how many more of these challenges I will need to face or to guess at how long this process will take. Instead, I am attempting to take it one day at a time, or occasionally even a minute or an hour at a time, as I prayerfully deal with each new adjustment. As daunting a task as this may be, at least I now have a track record of the months since Gayle's death to tell me that each new challenge can and will be handled with a measure of success.

Your adjustments

Adjustments have to be made almost immediately after the loss. Learning to cook, take care of regular maintenance on the house or car, sleep alone, or keep important documents straight can all be difficult. Seemingly small things can require major adjustments. It's all very difficult but also inevitable and necessary.

Few if any of the adjustments are easy. Every one is a reminder of your loss and the immense feelings of emptiness and loneliness that accompany it. But as you accomplish even the smallest of these changes, you can celebrate the fact that you may actually be a bit stronger than you previously thought.

Celebrate each new success regardless of how insignificant it may seem. One day at a time, one step at a time, you are making progress.

Some people may be concerned that celebrating a milestone in the process of grief may be disrespectful to the deceased. I would remind you that while your grief is, at first, a fitting tribute to your loved one, healthy grieving shifts from a tribute of grief to a new tribute that is found in living the life you still have to its fullest. In most cases, this is exactly how the deceased would want you to demonstrate your respect. Healthy grief will always take the griever to this point. A life well lived becomes the new tribute to the deceased. Therefore, celebrate your progress. Every adjustment is a step toward a healthier tribute to your loved one.

Adjustments

Exercises
1. Continue to keep a journal to log your memories, feelings, and experiences.
2. What adjustments have you had to make thus far?
3. What adjustments do you anticipate will be the most difficult?

Chapter 6
Surprises

Adjustments are tough, but surprises can feel like a 260-pound linebacker hitting you from your blind side. You hit the turf, the wind is knocked out of you, and your head reels as you try to get your bearings. The pain is indescribable! You wonder what just hit you.

While much in your experience of grief will come as a surprise, there are things you anticipate. I knew Gayle's birthday would be difficult, as would Thanksgiving, Christmas, our anniversary, and Valentine's Day. I also anticipated that the anniversaries of her first symptoms, hospitalization, diagnosis, death, and funeral would also be challenging. I knew that my first trips, first sermons, and the first time of recording new television shows would be hard to get through. I anticipated these things and was able to prepare for them.

Yes, those anticipated events were still quite painful; but I knew they would be, so I wasn't blindsided.

But every now and again, something surprises me. From time to time, I'm hit by something I hadn't anticipated, and it throws me for a loop. It may be a song on the radio, something a friend does or says, or finding an unexpected letter in a box of odds and ends. *Without warning, a flood of emotion overwhelms me, and I'm reduced to a quivering mass of Jell-O.*

One such surprise came when I did my taxes. It was the first time for me to file since Gayle's death. I use tax software that walks you through the process, but when I had to note that Gayle had died during 2016—when I had to check "deceased" for Gayle—I was surprised. That simple little check mark brought the tears.

Surprises

I hadn't anticipated that something so simple would set me off! The sudden flood of emotions ambushed me. This seemingly insignificant task almost left me paralyzed.

With the passing of time, I am surprised less often; and I realize I'm getting better with each new day. Joy is returning, hope is no longer a stranger, and I am functioning at a level that is closer to normal. Even so, there remains much work to be done. The big stuff hurts like crazy just as I knew it would. But these pesky little surprises cause an amazing level of pain. I really don't like surprises anymore!

You will be tempted to avoid things you anticipate will be painful. I know I am. But it is vital that you not run from pain. Pain is inevitable and necessary, if you are ever going to heal. Surprises can be unpleasant; but as we deal with each new episode of pain, we gain strength and make progress toward healing.

Devastating surprises

Some surprises are better than others. It is one thing to be surprised by a song at church, a line from a poem, or a story from a friend. These are normal and expected; and even though they may be initially painful, ultimately they can help you make progress.

But some surprises are devastating. I'm thinking of a woman who, after her husband's death, discovered that he'd had numerous affairs throughout their married life. They had been married for more than fifty years, and she had no idea that he had been unfaithful to her. When she made her discovery, it left her grieving more than her husband. She grieved the loss of the marriage she thought she had. In reality, her marriage had been something very different from what she had believed.

Her sorrow turned to rage! She told me she was intensely angry with her husband, the other women in his life, and even with herself for being so gullible. It took a very long time to accept this new reality, release her anger, and find healing. Such devastating surprises complicate mourning greatly.

Pleasant surprises?

Not all surprises are bad, however. A good friend and widow sent me a message. She lost her husband a few years before I lost Gayle, so she is further along in this process than I am. She reminded me that not all surprises are bad.

My friend told the story of some changes she is making in her home. In preparing for the arrival of carpet installers, she decided to clear out some things to make their job of moving furniture easier, and she ran across some documents her late husband had put away. She was surprised to find the documents—things like his private pilot's log—and was thrilled to see his handwriting. It was a surprise that brought a smile to her face, pleasant memories to mind, and a moment of joy.

My friend's story reminded me of pleasant surprises I have found since Gayle's passing. People who neither Gayle nor I had previously met have shared with me the positive impact Gayle had on their lives. Women in particular have shared that the beautiful, confident, Christian woman they watched on television inspired them to be better women.

Another surprise came when I was going through a few boxes in Gayle's closet. I found a letter that had been neatly tucked away for nearly forty years. It was a letter Gayle had written to God on the occasion of our second anniversary. Dated December 28, 1977, the letter listed what Gayle viewed as being my positive qualities. She thanked God for me, my positive attributes, and for the love we had for each other.

The letter was a pleasant surprise. I hadn't known of its existence, and finding it brought joy, gratitude, and a different kind of tears. It was a positive surprise indeed, but it still resulted in tears.

I know I will have many more surprises ahead. Some surprises will be negative and others positive. Right now, most surprises of both varieties result in weeping. But I am looking forward to the day when, like my friend, I will be moved to smiles with every pleasant surprise.

Exercises

1. What are the latest entries in your journal?
2. What has surprised you most about your loss?
3. Have you had any pleasant surprises? If so, what are they?

Chapter 7

Expectations and Criticisms

We tend to have our own expectations of where we should be and how quickly we should be making progress. Our family and friends have their own set of expectations. Differing expectations can make the trip really hard.

Here's a blog post I wrote on the subject:

"How are you doing?"

The honest answer is, "Really, really bad!"

But then again, I'm supposed to be doing really, really bad, so I suppose the best answer would be, "About as well as expected."

For the most part, knowing what the Bible teaches about death, resurrection and reunion does little to quell the pain. I know those things are true but they do nothing to bring Gayle back right now, and that's what I want. Knowing I'll see her again is wonderful, but it still hurts now.

Also, as a counselor and chaplain who has taught grief recovery and has experienced grief before, I know the symptoms I'm experiencing are normal. Knowing that does not diminish the symptoms. It only assures me that I'm normal. But then again, normal really stinks right now.

Many people who either are currently in fresh and deep grief, or have been there not long ago have contacted me. It's amazing to me how many of them thank me for being honest about how I feel. They tell me that a lot of people want to minimize their experience, or to ignore it altogether. That can add to a person's pain.

Tears to Joy

Grief is real and everyone experiences it at some point in their life. The really big losses in some measure never go away. They may dissipate over time, but they never truly go away. They remain until your own death, or resurrection and reunion. And that makes the Bible teachings dear to me.

So, how am I doing? About as well as can be expected.

Here is another blog post that expresses the idea of expectations. In the post, I tell the story of a phone call from someone at the hospice that cared for Gayle during her last few days.

I received a call the other day from someone at Faith Hospice. This is the organization that cared for Gayle in our home during her last few days. The lady asked how we were doing. Here's the conversation.

Me: We stink! But we stink appropriately. We are all sad and crying and feeling lost, but that's what's supposed to be happening right now.

Nice Lady: That's true.

Me: However, as I assess our situation I would say we are low risk grievers right now. We are all expressive of our pain and cry easily in front of each other. We give and receive support, talk openly about Gayle, normalize each other's feelings, and are very close as a family unit. Also, our faith has remained strong so I really think we are low risk right now.

Nice Lady: My jaw just dropped. I've been doing this a long time and no one has ever spoken those words to me. It sounds like I'm sitting in a team meeting for hospice with the social worker, nurses and chaplain. I mean, seriously, no one has ever said anything like this to me so I don't really know what to say.

Me: Well, I used to do your job. I was a hospice chaplain and also provided grief support for the families after a loss. And I'm a counselor and a minister.

Nice Lady: Wow! You learned your job well. You sure do practice what you preach.

Me: Gayle was a pastor. One of my daughters is a counselor and the other is a teacher who just switched jobs and is becoming a pastor. So I guess we all have careers that lend themselves to this sort of thing. As a family we're really close, and that helps. But mainly, our faith has been a real strength.

Expectations and Criticisms

Nice Lady: I can't wait to tell the team about our conversation! I called to cheer you up but you've cheered me up!

Me: Thanks for calling.

Nice Lady: No, thank you!

It was a fun conversation, really. It encouraged me to realize that while this really, really hurts, we're probably doing about as well as could be expected. Thank you Jesus!

Not all issues with expectations are as easy or entertaining as this. Some are much more difficult and more painful. The things that hurt most have to do with people who want to provide a quick fix to your problem, or those who criticize you for your expressions of grief.

For me, the vast majority of people were positive, loving, and longed to help. But in their attempts to help, even well-intentioned people can do or say things that cause discomfort. I know they love me and long for me to be happy, so it's difficult for me to be too hard on them since their motives are pure.

Even so, there were times after I wrote an expression of my grief and pain when at least a few people suggested something to the effect that Gayle would not want me to be this unhappy and that I need to remarry. I must state that I disagree with the aforementioned statement on at least two counts.

First, Gayle *would* have wanted me to be this unhappy, at least at that moment.

The average recovery time from a significant loss is one to two years; but even then, some experience of pain and sorrow will last a lifetime. Unhappiness, sorrow, and pain are normal and necessary experiences of grief. In fact, if you do *not* experience these things, it is likely that you are not grieving appropriately. Your failure to grieve in a healthy fashion will eventually exact a severe price from you. The rule of thumb is that you do better with grief if you grieve intensely and early. That includes feelings of sadness and genuine pain.

Therefore, since Gayle would ultimately want me to grieve in a healthy fashion while giving myself the best possible opportunity for a healthy recovery, she *would* want me to be this unhappy for as long as was necessary for my full recovery. She would want it because she would want me to be emotionally, physically, spiritually, and relationally healthy.

To state that I should not experience a certain level of pain suggests that grief is a competition. Those experiencing one sort of loss should only experience a certain level of pain, while those experiencing a different sort of loss should have another level of pain. I find this entire notion to be ludicrous.

Second, the statement implies that remarriage would be the cure for my sadness.

In addition to being a minister of the gospel, I am a trained counselor. I am trained and very experienced in both grief and marriage (although the two were not originally intended to go hand in hand). One of the things I have told people who want to get married is that marriage was never intended to fix your sadness, unhappiness, loneliness, sorrow, or brokenness. In fact, if you are currently unmarried and these words constitute an accurate description of your current state—do not get married! Please! Marriage will not fix these issues.

Marriage was designed for a joyful person who longs to share that joy with another joyful person. Marriage is to be a place to live out your shared goals, dreams, visions, and purposes. It is a way to enjoy a team ministry. Marriage is the perfect expression of shared joy!

During the first year after the loss, my dominant emotional state included sorrow, emptiness, loneliness, and sadness. It would have been inadvisable for me to remarry at that time. As these emotions subsided and joy once again became a more dominant force in my emotional landscape, remarriage became a possibility.

When you have lost a spouse and the day arrives when you would consider remarriage, your motivation to marry should be because you long to share your life, your ministry, and your joy with another human being. Until then, you should remain alone. God has seen you through this far, and I am fully confident He will continue to guide you through the weeks, months, and even years ahead.

Criticism

As I shared my journey though grief openly on Facebook, someone criticized those public expressions of pain, stating that I was seeking attention. This person said there were people who had far worse problems than mine and that I should be grateful I had experienced such a great marriage. This person told me that I should be glad I had my health and was employed.

While much of what she said was true, it was nonetheless hurtful to me. I have come to believe that the criticism grew out of a misconception of the process of grief. Grief is something that most people in North America

Expectations and Criticisms

and northern Europe do not handle very well. Strong expressions of negative emotions are frowned upon. They make most Caucasian Americans extremely uncomfortable. This is one of the reasons most Caucasian Americans handle grief so poorly.

Many people from other ethnic groups in the United States and abroad feel freer to express their pain. As such, they deal with their grief in much healthier ways than their Caucasian counterparts. Research corroborates this. Of course, these are rather broad generalizations and may not apply equally across the board, but I stand by the statements as being generally true.

My rather public expressions of sorrow were merely an attempt to deal with my pain in healthy ways. As a counselor, chaplain, and teacher of grief-recovery classes, I know what the research says and attempted to practice what I've always preached. Public expressions in no way should be viewed as seeking sympathy or as implying that one's loss and one's sorrow are any greater or deeper than another's. Nor should it imply to you that the life of the mourner is not blessed in spite of their loss. I was reminded of just how blessed I am by an incident late in Gayle's life.

When Gayle knew she was going to die, I asked her whether she was angry. Her answer was, in effect: "I've had sixty years of immaculate health while some people never get a single day. I've had forty years of a marvelous marriage and ministry while most people never know those joys. I've got wonderful children, grandchildren, extended family, and friends. Should I be angry that this lasted only sixty years and not eighty? That to me would seem to be ungrateful."

I echo Gayle's sentiments. My life has been and continues to be blessed beyond imagination. I have received blessings that most of the world will never know. I am *not* to be pitied.

But I have had a great loss. I am committed to grieving that loss in as healthy a fashion as I am capable. That includes, at times, public expressions of my pain.

Criticisms, even justified criticisms, are rarely helpful to anyone in grief. Whether or not this person's observations were accurate, they caused me a great deal of pain and did nothing to aid in my recovery. Therefore, I chose not to pay too much attention to the comments.

Overcontemplation of the expectations of others can destroy you. While it is important to listen to trusted voices during your time of mourning, it is not necessary to listen to purely critical voices.

Tears to Joy

When my uncle Fred passed away, his wife, Gladys, did not have a funeral and had Fred cremated. Those were his and her wishes.

My sister, Vicki, went to stay with Aunt Gladys after the funeral. Aunt Gladys told Vicki that some people in the church said she was wrong to have cremated Fred and wrong to not have a funeral. Aunt Gladys asked Vicki what she thought, and Vicki said she should do whatever made her comfortable. She further stated that it only mattered what she and Uncle Fred thought and felt. Those simple words helped Aunt Gladys feel better about her choices.

Additionally, holding unrealistic expectations for yourself can be just as destructive, if not more so. Above all, it's important to keep expectations low and learn to be gentle with yourself. *Grief is hard and takes time.*

Exercises
1. What expectations have others expressed about you and your process of grief? Have those expectations been helpful or harmful to you?
2. What expectations have you held for yourself? Are they realistic?

Chapter 8

Pace

Another problem is the fact that people grieve at different paces. This is one reason why the divorce rate is so high for couples who lose a child. Grief tends to isolate you, causing you to withdraw into yourself. Further, if the husband and wife grieve at different paces and one progresses faster than the other does, the result can be a very sharp division and severely hurt feelings.

If you have a family who is grieving the same person you are, then you cannot grieve solely at your own pace. Some things are doable at your pace, but others are not. *You must collaborate in your grief.*

There are some things I may be ready to do; but if my children or grandchildren are not ready, I won't do those things just yet. Of course, the reverse is true as well.

Also, there are other things I may not want to do, but my children or grandchildren need me to do those things. An example of that is decorating my home for Christmas. I'd just as soon skip it, but my grandchildren want the place decorated. So my daughters, accompanied by my grandchildren, decorated my home.

Another example of how we grieve at different paces can be seen in the way we deal with the deceased's property. I'm not big on possessions. My memories have little to do with the things we have. Therefore, I would prefer to simplify my life and divest myself of a lot of our possessions. An example might be crystal bowls, pitchers, and glasses. I do not entertain and have no need of those things. I would prefer that my children take what they want and

Tears to Joy

that I find appropriate ways to dispose of the rest. But my children may not be ready for me to do that yet. If I feel any resistance from them, I delay that process until we are *all* ready.

It's not really a big deal to postpone these processes, so I delay in order to make certain that the entire family can grieve at a pace that is comfortable for us all.

It doesn't hurt me to make the concessions. It actually helps my family when I am willing to accommodate their needs. They, of course, have done the same thing for me. In this way, we avoid the contentious divisions that happen so often after a loss and, instead, chart a healthier course for our grief as a family.

No one can tell you exactly how long your grief should last, nor can they tell you exactly when you should leave one phase of the journey and enter the next. Overall, most people endure intense grieving for one to two years. But that number isn't exactly written in stone. It is possible to move a bit more quickly than that or to take longer and still fall within the healthy range.

If others in your family or immediate social group are grieving the same loss but at a pace that differs from your own, it will be important for you to make accommodations. It is also important that you do not put pressure on yourself to grieve at a pace that is similar to theirs. *In short, grieve at the pace that feels right for you while allowing others to do the same.*

Exercises

1. Don't forget to write regularly in your journal. Remember to write your memories, feelings, and experiences.
2. If there are others close to you who are grieving the same loss, do you feel they are grieving faster, slower, or at about the same pace?
3. If they are grieving at a pace that is different from yours, does that concern you? Why or why not?

Chapter 9

Guilt

Now we move to the problem of guilt. This is one of the most difficult things to deal with on the journey of grief. Guilt can overwhelm you and truly impede your progress.

Guilt can emerge about things said or done and about things not said or done in the relationship. You can feel guilty that your loved one died and you are still alive, guilty about feeling good, or guilty about taking so long with your grief. Your feelings of guilt can be realistic or unrealistic.

I remember when someone said, "It's nice to see your smile again." While it felt good that my friend had said this, for just a split second I felt guilty. It was almost as though my smile—my momentary happiness—was a betrayal of Gayle's love.

I know it is silly. I realize that eventually as we grieve, joy returns. It doesn't return all at once, and it may never be like it once was, but it returns. And joy is more likely to return a little bit sooner if you've done the work of grieving properly. It helps if you grieve intensely and early. I know these things, and I've done these things. A part of the reason I did them was to facilitate health, healing, and eventually joy. But when joy, like Punxsutawney Phil, briefly poked its head out of the hole of grief, I felt guilty that spring could possibly be reemerging.

We grieve because we have loved. The greater we love, the greater we grieve. And truthfully, you never truly stop grieving for the rest of your life. But intense grieving should not last forever. Intense, depressing, crying-your-eyes-out, can't-get-out-of-bed-in-the-morning grief should eventually give way to a less virulent variety of sorrow. This is the way it is supposed to work.

Tears to Joy

When I was congratulated for my smile, I confronted my guilt. I questioned it and realized it was misplaced. I'm attempting to dispose of it.

Sorrow has not ended. But I do not need to feel guilty over joy's brief visit. And should I continue to do the hard work of grief, perhaps joy will once again become a permanent resident in my life.

I have determined that I will not complicate my grief by unneeded, misplaced guilt. Grief is hard enough by itself.

Another way guilt manifests itself is through something I'll call "false guilt." Guilt can be a good thing. If we harm someone or if we do something we know violates a code of ethics or our sensibilities of right and wrong, we truly *should* feel guilty. This form of guilt can move us to make amends and to extend apologies and expressions of sorrow for our actions, and most important, it can motivate us to change our behavior. Truthfully, if we don't feel guilty, we are unlikely to make positive changes.

What about those times when we feel guilt about something that is unrealistic? Consider the following example.

I spoke with a nurse whose husband died from cancer. As we spoke, she said, "I just feel so guilty!"

"Guilty? Why guilty?" I replied.

"I should have known it was cancer."

I asked, "How many different doctors did you take your husband to before you got your diagnosis?"

"Four," she answered.

I continued, "Did those doctors run blood tests, MRIs, CT scans, and other tests?"

"Well, yes, they did. They ran a lot of tests," she replied.

I asked, "And even with all those scans, X-rays, blood tests, biopsies, and examinations, how long did it take those four doctors to give you an accurate diagnosis?"

"From the first visit to a doctor to diagnosis was nearly six weeks," she answered.

I furrowed my brow and leaned in as I continued, "So four doctors, with all their training and experience and with all the medical technology and laboratories at their disposal, took nearly six weeks to figure out what was wrong with your husband, but you should have known? How could you expect that you would know?"

"I'm a nurse, and I'm his wife!"

Guilt

This woman was suffering from false guilt. It was unrealistic that she "should have known" that her husband had cancer. And even if she had known, there is some question as to whether the outcome would have been any different. I shared this with her and told her that the only way she could have known was for her to be God, and that job is already taken.

False guilt is damaging because there is nothing that can be confessed or changed. It is an overwhelming sense of responsibility and failure for something that is clearly out of your control. There is no release from this form of guilt other than to recognize it for what it is and then reject it.

False guilt impedes the grieving process, makes accepting reality more difficult, and tears down an already damaged self-esteem. Identifying and rejecting false guilt is important to the recovery process.

Exercises
1. Journal entries are important. Continue to think, write, talk, and cry.
2. Do you feel guilty? It may help to write about those feelings. What do you feel guilty about?
3. Can you tell whether these feelings of guilt are false guilt or true guilt? If you don't know for certain, it may help to ask someone whose opinion you trust.

Chapter 10

Awkwardness

A significant loss leaves you wondering exactly who you are. Your identity changes completely. You had seen yourself as a part of the person who died; and now that your loved one is gone, your identity shifts. But shifts to what?

It takes a while to figure this out, and until you do, you feel very much out of sorts. The best word that comes to mind is *awkward*. It's inadequate as a true descriptor of the feeling, but it will have to do for now.

The moment I lost Gayle, awkwardness began for me. I was at loose ends. My identity was gone. I had been Gayle's husband, friend, and coworker for more than four decades. Who was I now? Most of our friends were "couple" friends. The few times I've been with those friends it was obvious to me, at least, that I was the one who no longer "fit." I can't say whether my friends felt that way, but I certainly did. It was awkward.

Filling out forms, filing taxes, grocery shopping, Christmas shopping, birthdays, church socials, introductions, and more can carry either the occasional awkward moment or much worse. *The first few times you stumble across these situations, it almost makes your head swim. It feels as though you are having a bad dream from which you never seem to awaken.*

Family gatherings were different due to Gayle's absence. While her death affected everyone, I was the one most impacted by it and the one who experienced the biggest struggle in finding a new family identity without Gayle. Visiting Gayle's family felt odd. They did absolutely nothing to make me feel that way; in fact, they went out of their way to let me know that after more

Awkwardness

than forty years I was indeed a part of the family even without Gayle. But I felt a difference in identity, and it was, to say the least, awkward.

Even in my own family, babysitting the grandkids felt different for them and for me. Heading over to a daughter's home for a meal felt incomplete. And smiling for the camera when posing for family photographs was a real challenge.

Almost everything made me feel out of sorts. Going to church, preaching, social occasions, holidays, travel, and presenting marriage seminars all felt strange without Gayle. And don't get me started about living in a house without her. Sleeping in my bed and eating meals without Gayle—*awkward* is too tame a word!

As time passes, the feelings of being out of place ease somewhat. Of course, just as I think I'm getting used to things, I am surprised by a new situation that once again highlights the fact that my identity has changed dramatically, and the whole process starts over again.

Eventually, new identities are formed, new "normals" are learned, and new ways of relating become more comfortable. But this process is taking quite some time, and the feelings of awkwardness are still there. I truly long for a new normal to take over and show awkwardness the door! All this, I suppose, will come in time.

I have chosen to do the only thing I am able to do. I will continue to face awkward situations instead of avoiding them. I will face them, plan for them, and practice this process with every new awkward situation that presents itself.

Exercises

1. Continue to think, write, talk, and cry.
2. What awkward experiences have you had during your journey of grief?
3. What new identities and new normals are you finding?

Chapter 11

Loneliness and Community

Loneliness is an inescapable part of life. For those in grief, the loneliness can be crushing. This is especially true if the person you've lost was an important part of your everyday life.

Gayle and I were together almost twenty-four hours a day, seven days a week. It was rare that I traveled without her, rare that we didn't work as a team, and rare that we didn't relax and play together. When Gayle died, I was suddenly alone. My loneliness was as painful as it was inescapable.

My situation was made worse by my travel schedule. Gayle and I normally traveled anywhere from 180 to 220 days a year. That much travel made it nearly impossible to have much of a church community or to maintain the beautiful friendships we had been blessed with for most of our lives. We joked that neither of us could afford the other to die because it would leave the one remaining completely alone in the world. Our joke became a reality for me when Gayle died.

If you are experiencing loneliness, perhaps some of what I've learned through my own experience will be of some value. First, I've learned that loneliness is not simply a lack of contact with others. Loneliness is, at its core, a lack of contact with self. This was true for me.

When Gayle was alive, my self-identity was completely wrapped up in being a part of a couple. It was always "Mike and Gayle"—rarely just "Mike." I thought of myself more as a part of a couple than as purely an individual. Losing Gayle made me lose that part of my identity. I had to rediscover who I was as a single person.

Loneliness and Community

Rediscovering yourself takes place best in solitude. It is in solitude that we find the time to ask such questions as, Who am I? What is my purpose? What do I want out of life? And what goodness do I possess that I might share with others?

These questions help us to get in touch with self. This is not just the self we are; but perhaps more important, it is the self we long to become. Solitude gives us the opportunity to think, write, cry, pray, and meditate on Scripture. It is through these activities that we are most likely to find positive answers to our questions.

Next, I learned that loneliness is a passive state of mind. Loneliness, therefore, is best overcome through positive action.

The lonely person asks, Why can't I be with people who like me? How can I get some support? Why is my church or community so couples focused?

In order to change our lonely state, we must turn to new questions. We need to ask, What goodness do I possess that I might share with others? How can I be a blessing to someone today? Who needs my love and support?

These are positive questions that imply the need to invest in the lives of others. Instead of wondering why no one invests in us, we choose rather to invest in people. In this way, we are able to positively combat our loneliness.

One of the best places to do this is in church. Finding a community of like-minded believers is one of the healthiest things you can do. At church, we will find people who can benefit from the investment we are willing to make in them. We also can find people who long to invest themselves in those in need. Investing in the lives of others brings a deeper meaning to life. It enhances life's joy and beauty.

Additionally, I chose to reconnect with friends via electronic means. While this was not the same as face-to-face communication, it was nonetheless invaluable to me. My travel schedule made electronic communication the best available option.

Through these means, I was able to share my life and to learn about the lives of my friends. I was also able to offer comfort, support, and understanding whenever needed. I chose to give of myself to others via email, Facebook, Twitter, cell phone, and more. I chose to invest in the lives of others, and that investment has paid dividends.

Loneliness is a passive state of mind. It must be overcome through active means. But the first step is to rediscover self through solitude.

Tears to Joy

Exercises
1. Are you experiencing loneliness? If so, what active means are you taking to combat your loneliness?
2. Schedule some time alone so that you can focus on rediscovering self. Prayerfully ask the questions I've suggested in this chapter.
3. Make plans to give of yourself to others.
4. Continue to think, write, talk, and cry.

Chapter 12
Crosswinds, Sorrow, and Joy

When you lose someone you love, you feel as though you are caught in the midst of a horrific storm. But just when it feels you will be drowned by the floodwaters, things begin to change. Sometimes they change for the better, sometimes for worse; and sometimes the change is simply a brief lull that is followed by winds of even more intense fury.

For so long, the only winds that blew in my life were the hurricane-force winds of grief. The winds would knock me down, pick me up, slam me against trees and walls, then start the entire process all over again. Nothing was protected from the winds. My work, social life, family life, busy time, down time, travel, holidays—every aspect of life was affected by the winds of grief.

As time passed, the force of the winds slowed a bit. The occasional gust still had a devastating effect, but the winds became a bit more manageable as I learned to lean against them while maintaining a sense of balance.

Later, there were days when the winds subsided, giving way to gentle breezes from another direction. These were the breezes of hope. Ever so slightly, the breezes brought hope for a renewed ability to concentrate and function, hope that my pain would not always be this intense, and hope that nuances of joy might return.

Then I learned that the calm in the storm was simply the eye of the hurricane. As we approached the first anniversary of Gayle's death, those winds picked up speed again. The entire family was affected. Depression increased, tears flowed more readily, anxiety grew, and sleep was a bit less satisfying.

The weeks surrounding the first anniversary of Gayle's death were once again stormy. But I continued to attempt to lean into the pain in an effort to truly deal with things rather than run from them. This strategy has served me well thus far, and I believe it will continue to be of value throughout all of grief's storms.

But if previous experiences are any indicator, I know that as I emerge from every new wave of grief, I will once again feel the gentle breezes of hope.

I want to live again. I want joy again. I hope for both. I long for a return of the gentle breezes. But the storm winds blow, change directions, and then stop for a while, only to begin again. Things change and yet remain the same.

The same dichotomy can be found in emotions. Tears give way to laughter, only to be replaced by tears. Despair, hope, panic, and numbness can be felt all within the course of a couple of hours.

At times, the most troubling thing is the tendency to feel two conflicting emotions almost simultaneously.

Sorrow and joy

Is it possible to hold sorrow and joy in your heart at the same time? I believe it is. Further, I believe it is necessary to do so in order to live fully.

Sorrow is an inescapable part of the human existence. One need not live long before one has a strong visitation of sorrow. In some cases, the sorrow is so strong, so pervasive, it seems to define our life.

The sorrow I feel over Gayle's death is a part of the fabric of my everyday existence. It is the backdrop behind the continuing story of my life. Yet my life's story is not *only* sorrow. I continue to find joy in life. Joy comes daily through the laughter of my grandchildren, the comfort of my family, the love of a dear friend, the exultation of worship, and the peace that comes through prayer. Every day is a strange mixture of sorrow and joy.

In the beginning, I felt guilty with every fleeting moment of joy. It seemed to be disrespectful to Gayle, or even a betrayal of my love for her. Fortunately, those feelings have given way to a deeper understanding.

Both sorrow and joy are essential elements to a full life. Since deep sorrow rarely leaves completely, we must learn to embrace both sorrow and joy simultaneously or we will have one and not the other.

Sorrow teaches us to hold dear the things of true value since they can be taken from us at any time. The knowledge of the fragility of these things causes us to hold dearly each moment, guard how we handle treasures, celebrate each experience with friends and family, breathe deeply of fresh air, bask fully

Crosswinds, Sorrow, and Joy

in sunshine, gaze in amazement at green trees and grass, rejoice over deep sleep, savor great food, and fully live every experience of life. While we never forget that which was lost, we are faithful to celebrate that which remains.

My love for God and my love for Gayle have brought me to a renewed commitment. I vow to *live* my life fully. I pledge to feel the depths of sorrow even as I love deeply, laugh with total disregard for propriety, minister with the fierce love of Christ, sing off-key with gusto, and dance embarrassingly for joy. I vow, by the mercies of Christ and with loving respect for Gayle, to live fully!

Sorrow and joy have kissed. Each is an essential element to life here and now. But one day, only joy will remain. How I long for that day!

Exercises

1. Remember to continue to think, write, talk, and cry.
2. What changes have occurred in your experience with grief? Have there been ups and downs? What were they like?
3. What conflicting emotions have you experienced? Can you see that experiencing a full range of emotions is necessary for a full life?

Chapter 13

Tears

A very dear friend sent me a message in which she commented how some cultures embrace visible expressions of grief (e.g., tears and loud crying), while other cultures discourage such displays. In the United States, in particular, the African American culture is very open to more visible expressions of grief. This is very unlike most Caucasian cultures in the United States, which prefer a more stoic approach. In reality, the African American community has it right in this regard.

This stoic approach to grief is fortified by a misguided belief that tears, crying, and even wailing in one's sorrow are a betrayal of faith. Quite the opposite is true. Tears are never discouraged on this earth. We are told that they will be wiped away in heaven (Revelation 21:4); but we are not in heaven yet, so wailing can be a perfectly appropriate activity here.

I remember an incident years ago when I was working as a hospital chaplain. I was called in to the emergency room (ER) late one night because an African American woman had been brought in with a severe heart attack. Her family was sitting in the family room of the ER. I ministered to the family as I checked in on the progress in the ER. It was obvious that the woman would soon die.

As I watched her family, I saw a lot of gentle touches between the members as well as open displays of tears. I realized that when this woman died, her family was likely to give loud expression to their pain. I then looked at the staff on duty that evening in the ER. They were all Caucasian. So I told the staff, "When this woman dies, her family is likely to be vociferous with their expressions of pain. If you are uncomfortable with such displays, you will need to cut them a wide swath. I will be present with the family, comforting the family and attempting to normalize their experience. If you can't do that or if you are simply uncomfortable with such loud expressions of grief, you'd better find a place to hide!"

The woman died, and true to my expectation, the family gave loud expression to their pain. Having earned their confidence, I was able to embrace each person as they cried. It was *loud*! I happened to look around the ER and could not see one of the Caucasian staff members. Culturally, this was foreign to them and caused them great discomfort. Yet what the family was able to do was actually very healthy.

Tears are healing. They are necessary. Don't be afraid to allow your tears to flow. The day will come when all tears are wiped from your eyes by the only *One* who is capable of doing so—Jesus Christ, the Resurrection and the Life; but until then, we have the gift of tears.

Exercises

1. Are you able to share your grief publicly through tears and other outward expressions of grief?
2. Continue to think, write, talk, and cry.

Chapter 14
Good Days, Bad Days, and Hope

Hope is a dangerous thing.
—Frank Darabont, *The Shawshank Redemption*

You know you're making progress when you begin having more good days than bad days. At first, there were no good days, but a few good moments. Through the weeks and months, there was a slow, almost imperceptible change from a few good moments to a few good hours to a good day every now and then. There have been setbacks as well as starts and stops, but overall there has been slow progress toward more and more good days.

For a time, there is guilt over feeling good. But eventually, reason wins out over those feelings, and you realize that it's all a part of the process. Joy begins to return in small measure.

If you are progressing, you are able to concentrate a bit more than before, and you may even have hope—hope for the future, hope that you can once again truly enjoy life, and hope that your life is not in some sense over.

The journey is not over by any measure. There are still milestones to pass. You are likely dreading many of those milestones. But your past successes should give you a renewed confidence that in spite of how difficult the anniversaries will be, you will yet survive and emerge with restored energy and hope.

Have no illusions. Know your life will never be the same. This is true for me as well. Your loved one cannot be replaced.

For me, Gayle is irreplaceable. I shall not try. But I now believe that life can still be good. It will be very different, and there will always be a hole in my life

Good Days, Bad Days, and Hope

where she once resided, but my life can once again be good.

Right now, I have good days and bad days with the good slightly outnumbering the bad. And tomorrow brings with it new challenges and renewed sorrows. But somewhere on the distant horizon, there exists a slight glimmer. I have identified the glimmer as hope.

Exercises

1. Are you having good days and bad days? Or perhaps your experience is more like good hours and bad hours. All of this is normal.
2. Do the good times give you a glimmer of hope? Where do you find hope in your life?
3. Continue to think, write, talk, and cry.

Chapter 15

Holidays and "Firsts"

When grieving, nights are usually harder than days, weekends more difficult than weekdays, and birthdays, anniversaries, and the holidays are the pits! While nothing will change that, you can usually make these occasions a little more manageable if you have a plan.

Make sure you limit your exposure to difficult scenarios by having an out. Have a plan to leave early if you so choose. During the holidays, attend fewer events, choosing perhaps those that may tend to be the least volatile. Keep to a schedule, but don't make the schedule too tight. Give yourself some leeway, and again, have an out. I had to remember this during the first Christmas season.

Gayle loved Christmas! She looked forward to it, planned for it, decorated for it, enjoyed the music, usually found a community sing-along for Handel's *Messiah* to participate in, did her best to plan special events for whichever church we attended, and planned something special for the family. Family get-togethers were filled with food, fun, spirituality, and laughter. Gayle was a gracious hostess and loved to entertain. She simply adored Christmas!

For our first Christmas without Gayle, my daughters and I decided to do something different. In the future, we will move the center for celebrations from my house to one of their houses. It seems to me that this only makes sense. But that first year we needed something to sort of break the ice, if you will.

So on Christmas Day, I used frequent flier miles to take both of my daughters, my son-in-law, two grandchildren, and myself to New York City. We came to see the lights and the sites of historical interest and to get away for a bit.

I am fortunate to have the miles from my travel for ministry. It is a real bonus

Holidays and "Firsts"

for me—and they came in handy for our first Christmas without Gayle.

We chose to do things that helped us celebrate the holidays in a way that was different from anything we've ever done. This helped relieve some of the tension and averted some of the pain. It was a blessing for the family. In future years, we will celebrate in a more traditional way; but for our first Christmas without Gayle, this made sense to us.

Three days after Christmas of 2016, December 28, marked forty-one years from the day I married Gayle. On that day, we saw the Statue of Liberty in the morning, then checked out of our hotel and headed for the airport and back to Dallas. It kept me busy enough to make it through the day without feeling too sorry for myself.

The key for me has been to have a plan. My plan may be different from your plan. What works for me may not work at all for you. But have a plan.

You should set modest goals for your first time through the holidays. Perhaps mere survival is a lofty enough goal! Sometimes the best goals are the most basic. Survival ranks among the most important goals when one is grieving.

Grief has a way of reducing and compressing everything. Our lofty aims are reduced to the most basic goal of mere survival. Long-term planning is compressed from the five- or ten-year plan to the five- or ten-hour plan. Sometimes the five- or ten-minute plan works too! As modest as this seems, it may be the best you can do as you deal with your losses.

The losses of your life have left you wounded and bleeding. The pain is intense, and the loneliness almost unbearable. And the thought of Thanksgiving and Christmas is odious.

If this describes you, then here are a few suggestions:

First, make the holidays about someone other than yourself. The first Christmas without Gayle was my year to truly focus on my grandchildren. In the past when I've faced a painful holiday season, I made the celebration about people in need and directed more of my financial resources toward making their holidays more enjoyable.

Second, remember the religious aspects of the holidays. Thanksgiving is an opportunity to give thanks. This forces you to remember that you still have much for which to give thanks. It helps you to focus on what you still have rather than on what you've lost. Likewise, Christmas is an opportunity to give thanks for the greatest Gift ever given.

Third, manage your time. Find opportunities to celebrate, but limit that time. If you need to leave a family gathering or even leave a Christmas concert

Tears to Joy

or worship service early, that's OK. You may decide to participate in fewer parties or events. That's OK too. Take control and manage things so that you can survive this first time through the holidays without the person you love.

Fourth, give yourself permission to cry without shame. It's going to happen, so be prepared. Bring tissues, warn those around you, and realize that this is not a sign of weakness but an acknowledgment that the love you have lost is a great love!

Fifth, make sure you have someone you can call or talk with when you need to. Don't bottle things up inside. Have a safe place to release. Talk to someone who understands and cares about you.

Finally, you may decide to do something of significance to remember and honor the person you have lost. Make a donation in your loved one's memory, plant a tree, or do something else that will be a lasting tribute to this person.

But whatever you choose to do, make sure you have an out if you need one. In the event that you try to do too much and become overwhelmed by the emotions, it might be best to know that you can extricate yourself from the situation. Make certain you can leave and retreat to a place of safety with fewer strong memories and emotions.

Years ago, while we were serving as pastors in Arlington, Texas, Gayle was instrumental in instituting an annual Thanksgiving dinner for the congregation. The Saturday before Thanksgiving people would bring their best china and silverware to set tables in the church's fellowship halls. Reservations were made so that everyone would be assured of having a seat at the event. The church provided most of the meal and organized the tables. It was always a wonderful time of fellowship and celebration as well as an opportunity to reach out to the community with invitations to attend the feast. Gayle and her team worked very, very hard every year to make sure the food was perfect, the halls beautifully decorated, and the program flawless. She did this for years until we left, but I believe it is a practice that continues in Arlington.

When our daughters became adults and moved to Dallas, with the help of their mother they instituted this same practice at the Dallas First Church of Seventh-day Adventists. Every year we had to make sure we were not traveling that weekend so that Gayle could assist her daughters in putting on this marvelous event. The Dallas church continued that tradition the first Thanksgiving after her death.

I walked into the gym at the Dallas First Church of Seventh-day Adventists that first Thanksgiving season without Gayle and saw the tables beautifully

Holidays and "Firsts"

set. The lighting and decorations had transformed the gym into an elegant banquet hall. Music was playing in the background. The scene was perfect.

I walked up and down the rows of tables, examining each one, and as I did, my memories overwhelmed me. I began to cry and was unable to stop. So I made my excuses and left.

This is an example of trying to do too much. I at least gave myself an out. I left when it was too much to take. As such, I do not view this as a failure but as an example of a successful plan. I tried to attend; but when I became overwhelmed, I was able to leave.

If you have had a significant loss in recent months or even years, you, too, will need to make decisions about how much is too much. Choose some things to attend and enjoy, but exclude others. And always give yourself an out!

As the years pass, I hope to be able to resume a more normal approach to the holidays. While they will never be the same, they can still be meaningful. But the first year was quite different. It was my goal to simply survive that first year.

During the first Christmas season, I attended the Christmas program for the elementary school where my granddaughter attended kindergarten. The children all did a fantastic job. I was proud of them all, but I was, of course, especially proud of my granddaughter. She was very focused on the task at hand. She sang with gusto and followed her teacher's direction closely. I enjoyed her enthusiasm for music, Jesus, and Christmas.

Of course, there was someone missing from the evening. Gayle would have simply adored the night. She would have been smiling from ear to ear as she watched Anna's performance. And after it was over, she would have told Anna how very proud she was to have her as her granddaughter. I smiled as I watched Anna's every move, cheered for her, and told her how much I loved her and how proud I was of her. It wasn't Grammy, but Papa did in a pinch.

A few nights before that Christmas program I attended the fourth birthday party of my grandson, Anderson. Again, there was someone missing. Gayle would have doted on Anderson and laughed and smiled as she helped him celebrate four years of life.

Instead, I bought Anderson's present (with much-appreciated help from my daughters) and wrote on his birthday card. I cheered him on and told him how much I loved him and how proud I was of him. It wasn't Grammy, but Papa did in a pinch.

Two more "firsts" were in the books. *With every "first," there is fresh pain.*

Tears to Joy

With every celebration of life, there is a corresponding grief for that which was lost. Sweet mixed with bitter. Joy even amid tears.

School programs, birthdays, Christmases, anniversaries, and more—each event challenges my strength and courage. And yet each success reminds me that as difficult as this is, it is doable!

A short time after these celebrations, my family attended the ground breaking for a new youth complex at the Arlington Seventh-day Adventist Church in Arlington, Texas. We attended because the building was named for Gayle: the Gayle Tucker Youth Annex.

Gayle loved children, youth, and young adults. She gave so much of her life to ministering to the young! We are honored that the Arlington church would name the building after her and wouldn't have missed the ground breaking for the world. Yet it, too, was a painful event.

Every "first" and every event that honors Gayle's memory is a reminder of just how rich life can be. I would not grieve had my life not been so full to begin with. And every tribute in Gayle's memory is a reminder of the life she lived so fully and the many people who were blessed so richly by that life. My pain comes from the richness of her life and of our life together.

So I say thank You, God! Thank You for each celebration and each fresh dose of pain. Thank You for having given me a life so rich and full that losing a part of it could be so incredibly painful! And thank You for giving me the strength to endure and even grow through this experience.

Exercises

1. What "firsts" have you experienced thus far?
2. What "firsts" are yet to come for you?
3. As the holidays approach, make a plan for your celebration. While making certain you enjoy the season, be sure not to overdo it. Always provide an out for yourself should you find you need one.

Chapter 16

Character of God

I am convinced that an essential element to the grief process is a proper understanding of the character of God. Losing a loved one is one of the most traumatic experiences of life. It's hard enough to get through the excruciating pain without complicating that pain with anger toward God.

Anger with God occurs when we think God owes us more than He has given us. It happens when we believe God has acted arbitrarily or unjustly. It may occur if we view God as having a punitive attitude or even a calloused disinterest. Such views result in anger toward the Sovereign Lord.

Anger with God takes a lot of energy, which is a commodity in short supply for most caught in the throes of grief. But it gets worse. It has been my observation that the vast majority of those directing anger toward God eventually turn their anger inward. God-focused anger slowly becomes self-anger. We turn our anger inward. "Anger turned inward" is a classic definition of depression. Therefore, wrong perceptions of the character of God eventually result in anger turned inward.

Another complication is our inability to make sense of the loss. The question "why" is frequently asked; and if we hold a distorted picture of God, our answer will result in additional pain. It is difficult enough when our understanding of God's character is healthy; but when we have a distorted picture of God, we can be in deep trouble.

Distortions come in many forms. On one hand, there is the distant, disinterested God or even the impotent God. Either God is so far removed from us that He doesn't care what happens or He is so weak that He is helpless to do anything about our suffering. These distortions can be crippling.

On the other hand, a God who chooses to send a loss in order to "test" you or "purify" your character is not a trustworthy God. If the death of your loved one was an attempt to punish either of you, we again have a picture of God that is harmful to our recovery.

How about these distortions?

- God is choosing another flower for His garden, so He chose to take your loved one.
- God is working out things for a greater good, such as the salvation of a lost soul, that requires the death of the person you hold dear.
- God is sending a warning message to all who choose to rebel against Him.
- God is simply refusing to fulfill His promises to you.

Distortions occur when we see God as distant and aloof or harsh and arbitrary. They occur when you view God as making it difficult for you to be saved by requiring meticulous obedience to rules that are arbitrary and myopic. *Any distortion of the truth about God increases the likelihood of complicated mourning.*

So what is the truth? I like what one person said: "The truth about God is that He is infinitely better than we have ever dared dream possible." (I heard that said decades ago and cannot find the author. So I share it without giving appropriate credit. But I believe it to be a concise statement of truth.)

God is loving, kind, long-suffering, merciful, gentle, good, and intimately concerned with the details of your life. He is infinitely bigger than we could ever dream possible, so we are unable to understand everything He does. Our failure to comprehend God does not mean He is bad. It means His goodness is beyond our comprehension.

All this is revealed to me in a unique theological concept called the great controversy. This is the metanarrative of Scripture. It is the story of a good God who created a perfect world with perfect beings. That perfect world was destroyed when evil entered the heart of one of God's created beings—an angel named Lucifer. This was always a possibility because God did not create robots that did not possess the option of refusing to return His love. True love always carries with it the potential for rejection. God made Himself vulnerable by allowing the work of His hand to be able to choose to reject Him. This happened in Lucifer's heart. He rejected the love of God.

Lucifer's rebellion spread to God's new creation on planet Earth. Our first parents joined the rebellion; and from that day until now, bad things happen to good people. Why? Because God is the Source of everything good. When we remove ourselves from the Source, we run the risk of bad things happening. Paradise has been lost, and that places everyone at risk.

God loved His creation too much to allow this separation to last forever. At great cost to Himself, God sent His Son, Jesus, to pay the penalty for sin and reconcile fallen man. Now all who accept that reconciliation will experience Paradise restored on the day Jesus returns to take us home.

The story of Scripture is a play in three acts: Paradise created, Paradise lost, and Paradise restored. Until Paradise is completely restored, bad things will continue to happen to good people. We have never been promised anything other than that. God has promised to love, accept, forgive, save, and give us a meaningful life here on Earth. He has further promised that this life is but a shadow of that which is to come. Ultimately, eternal life will be ours. And it is in *that* life that all sickness, sin, sorrow, and loss will be forever banished.

In the meantime, we are loved with a love too great for human comprehension. God is crazy about us and longs for us to be happy! That is the truth about God as I see it.

Holding a correct image of God enables us to endure the vicissitudes of life as we await His return. It helps us to endure the unendurable. Our pain is not complicated by anger with God. We realize that God has been faithful to us, giving us even more than He had promised. We are loved, accepted, forgiven, and reconciled, and we will eventually be given eternity in a place where no one ever dies. Whether we've enjoyed life for eighty years or eighty days, we realize that God has been faithful. Our pain is, therefore, not complicated by misplaced anger.

I believe my grief has been made a bit lighter due to this accurate picture of God and His character. That picture has enabled me to experience grief uncomplicated by anger, and it allows me to recognize and accept gifts of comfort that God sends me. Seeing God as loving and viewing Him in the context of the great controversy has made all the difference for me.

Exercises

1. How would you describe your view of God?
2. Has your concept of God helped or hurt your journey through grief?

3. How has your view of God changed through your loss?
4. If your view of God is negative, are you interested in changing that view?
5. Take active steps toward a more positive picture of God. Make an appointment with a pastor or counselor who sees God as loving. Read books about God by Philip Yancey, Max Lucado, or others.

Chapter 17
Anger With God—Part 1

Living on in faith after the death of a loved one is difficult. It always has been and always will be. Getting your mind around the loss and how it changes your view of God is a large part of what makes staying behind so difficult.

In my previous losses, there came a time when it was apparent to me that there were two issues I was dealing with. One was the pain and grief of the loss itself. The second was the complicating, time-consuming, energy-sapping experience of my anger with God. A part of that anger was made worse by my seeming inability to get an answer from Him, hear from Him at all, or make sense of what had happened. In time, the anger almost outweighed the pain of the loss itself. It dominated or, at the very least, colored every emotion.

I determined that I would need to deal with the anger first if I was ever to totally deal with, and eventually accept, the loss. *What I did was helpful for me. It may not be for you.* It may sound ludicrous to you. If so, please regard it as well intentioned but not useful.

I decided to make some basic assumptions. *First assumption, God really is good.* The alternative to that assumption is to live in a universe that is so unthinkably cruel, chaotic, and destructive as to offer absolutely no hope. I had to make another assumption. I had to assume that God was basically good even though I did not understand what He had done.

Second, I had to assume that since God was basically good and wanted good things for me and the person I had lost, *the real issue was not with what God had done but with my understanding of what He had done.* In fact, God is so much higher than I am that it was highly unlikely that I would ever understand it.

Tears to Joy

Therefore, it seemed to me that the only reasonable way for me to deal with my issues of anger with this untouchable, unreachable God was to simply forgive Him. Strange as that may seem, I decided that the only way to resolve my deep feelings of anger and resentment was to trust that He actually did have a plan that I simply didn't understand; therefore, I could simply choose to forgive Him in order to release my negative emotions.

Having done this, eventually I was free to focus on the loss itself. I feel the pain of the loss without the complicating emotion of anger with God—an anger that left no other possible resolution. I felt the emotion of loss, the grief, the pain, the absence of that person in my life, and I grieved it all.

I was able then to grieve in a healthier, purer manner. While I still do not understand the whys of anything much that happens here, if I make the basic assumption that somewhere, somehow there really is a plan in place by a loving God who wants what is best for me, my forgiving Him makes life easier and happier.

To assume anything else is to doom myself to an unhappy, pointless existence for the rest of my life. I feel there has to be a better way to live, so I have chosen another course. It is working for me and helps me grieve more purely without the complications of unresolvable anger.

I have no idea if any of this is of value to you at all. It may not be. But it has been a lifesaver for me. My pain for Gayle's loss is just that—pain for the loss—and has no complications of anger. I have simply chosen to make a few difficult but helpful assumptions, to forgive God for not making those reasons available to me, and then to move forward. That works for me. I pray that if this doesn't work for you, you will find something that truly does help.

I don't think I will ever know the reason why, if there is such a reason. But for me, that's OK. Since it's unknowable anyway, not knowing has to be placed in a context that is somewhat acceptable. This practice makes that possible.

That's all. It may be silly. It may not help. It may even feel insensitive. If so, please forgive me. I can only share with you my experience.

Exercises

1. Are you experiencing anger with God over your loss? How do you plan to deal with your anger?
2. Are you able, in spite of your unanswered questions, to make the assumption that God is good and only wants the best for you? Can you see a value to the process of your grief in making such an assumption?

Chapter 18
Anger With God—Part 2

As a pastor, I have always rejected the notion of the gospel of prosperity. This is the teaching that if you will give God a seed gift of five dollars today, soon He will give you twenty dollars. It is the notion that God rewards our faithful gifts and service with financial blessings and the blessing of a better and happier life. Truthfully, I see no biblical support for such a teaching and believe that many who teach this do so in order to increase donations to their own ministries or, worse yet, their own pockets.

I know of many people who reject the theology in principle, but they tend to practice it in reality. I must confess that I was one of those people. Allow me to explain.

During the mid- to late-1980s, I pastored a church in Texas without receiving a salary. At the time, I was involved with my family's business, and our financial needs were being met. I didn't need a salary from the church, so I pastored for about seven years without receiving one.

Throughout those years, that church grew tremendously. Attendance grew from about two hundred to five hundred per week, our school grew, and we went through three different building and remodeling projects in order to have enough room. Since our financial needs were met through the family business, Gayle and I gave 30 percent of our gross income in tithes and offerings. It was a grand time for our family and for the church.

Then something terrible happened. The full story would take too long to tell here, but suffice it to say that through no fault of my own, we lost our home and our savings, and our income was cut by 70 percent. Again, I had done nothing wrong, but it appeared to me that my ministry had ended, and I would likely never preach again.

Some of you may be wondering what could cause such a dramatic turn of events. I must appeal to you to simply trust that I'm telling the truth. The full story would leave you scratching your head and would take too much of this book to tell.

My immediate reaction was to become very angry with God. At this time in my life, anger was always my go-to emotion whenever things went badly, and this experience was no exception. I was faced with multiple losses, and I was angry. I lost my reputation, ministry, job, savings, home, and any sense of security I might have had. As a result, I became very angry with God.

In my anger, I employed sarcasm in my prayers. I said, "So what did You want, God? Did You want me to give forty percent of my gross income? Should I have worked even harder and given even more hours for free? Should the church have grown faster? Seriously! What did You want?"

The classic definition for depression is "anger turned inward." Well, that's exactly what happened. My anger turned inward, and I became severely depressed. I was never treated for depression but somehow managed to stagger through day after day. But boy was I depressed and angry!

My depression was finally relieved after thirteen years! Although I have still not recovered financially, my fortunes turned around significantly at that time. As things improved, I realized that not only was I still preaching, my ministry had a wider influence than I could have ever dreamed previously. My finances were greatly improved, and my reputation was better than ever.

It was then that I began to analyze my long years of depression and anger with God. As I did, I came to a very humbling conclusion. *My anger with God came when I believed God owed me more than He had given me.* I became angry when I felt my sacrifice of time, talent, and money deserved a better response from God. In essence, I had subconsciously expected the gospel of prosperity. God "owed" me because of my good works and financial generosity.

Then I began to analyze exactly what God truly had promised me and found that God had never promised the things I expected from Him. God has promised to love, accept, forgive, and redeem me. He has promised to give me a life of meaning and purpose, to walk with me through every dark valley (a promise in itself that implies I would indeed walk through "dark valleys"), and to eventually give me eternal life. Only then would I receive unimaginable happiness, uninterrupted success, and eternal life. None of those things are guaranteed here on this planet during this lifetime. God had given me everything He had promised and much, much more! I was angry that those "unpromised" blessings had not lasted longer.

When I realized that my anger with God had been misplaced—when I had to admit that I was attempting to hold God responsible for things He had never promised me—I confessed my sin to God and asked for His forgiveness. Then I asked that God would make my "lived" theology congruent with my "preached" theology. I asked that He help me never again to be angry with Him for failing to provide me with things He had never promised to give.

Now fast-forward nearly thirty years to the day Gayle received the diagnosis of terminal cancer. In my former days, I would have responded with rage against God. I would have been unspeakably angry with God for taking my godly wife away from me. But much to my surprise, I experienced absolutely no anger when I learned of Gayle's diagnosis. Instead, I felt only gratitude. I was grateful for the blessings I had experienced for so many years.

God has done for me the very thing I had asked Him to do. He had made my lived theology congruent with my preached theology. I was not angry with God for failing to continue my wonderful blessings. I was instead grateful for that which I had received. And to this day I have not been angry with God for this loss.

I have no idea whether my story resonates with you. It may be that my experience in no way parallels yours. If so, please simply take this as an interesting story and leave it there. But if my story in some way reminds you of your experience, perhaps there is something here for you to learn as well. And if you learn the lessons I learned, perhaps those lessons will help you deal with any anger you might feel toward God.

This is my hope and prayer for you.

Exercises

1. If you are angry with God, is it possible that at least some of that anger comes from a subconscious belief that God somehow owes you more than He has given you? Could it be that you believe God should have continued to bless you through the life of the person you loved?
2. If your answer to the above question is Yes, what do you plan to do with this revelation?
3. It might be helpful for you to journal about your anger with God. What lies at its root? Is your anger based on faulty beliefs or expectations?

Chapter 19

Anger With and/or Guilt About the Deceased

There are times when the anger you feel is anger with the person who died. The same can be true of feelings of guilt. These can be difficult to resolve since the deceased is not able to respond to your efforts at reconciliation. How should you proceed?

My suggestion is simple. Write a letter to the deceased. Now I realize that many of you will find this to be a curious thing to do; but if you hear me out, I think you may find it to be helpful.

Anger

If you are angry with the person who died, state the reasons for your anger in the letter. Write the letter as if the deceased would receive it well, and be perfectly honest. This may not have been true if the person was still alive; but since the person is not, you can write the letter as if he or she would receive it well. State specifically what the person has done to make you angry, and share exactly how this has negatively impacted your life. Share emotions, the negative results of the deceased's actions, and more. Be very detailed in your letter.

Also, state how this action has affected your emotions toward the deceased. If it has made you angry or hurt, state that. If you are resentful or even longing for revenge, state that. If the person's behavior has caused you to love him or her less, share that in the letter as well. Be perfectly honest.

Then state in the letter that in spite of what was done, in spite of how this

Anger With and/or Guilt About the Deceased

action has negatively impacted your life, and even in spite of how this has affected your feelings toward the deceased, you have decided to forgive him or her. State specifically the words *I forgive you*. Realize that no one actually deserves forgiveness. If the person deserved it, he or she wouldn't actually need it! *You deserve the freedom and relief that comes from forgiving this person, so that is why you choose to do it.*

After you've written the letter, it may be helpful to actually do something with it. You may choose to attach it to a helium-filled balloon and then, after some prayer or ceremony of your own choosing, release the balloon as though you are sending it heavenward. It is now no longer your issue. It now belongs to God, and you have no right to hold on to the resentment. You've given it away.

Others choose to create or decorate a box, which they name their "God box." After writing the letter, they place it in the God box, indicating that they are giving the matter to God. Whenever they are tempted to relive the emotions of that pain, they refuse to do so because this issue now belongs to God. It is no longer their possession.

Guilt

If you feel guilty about something you have done to the deceased, write a letter to the deceased. State what you did, said, or failed to do or say that you deem to be inappropriate. Ask for forgiveness from the deceased, and imagine that person saying the words *I forgive you*. Then take the same issue and tell God about it. Imagine God saying the same words, *I forgive you*.

You may dispose of the letter by burning it after a ceremony or prayer of your own making, or you may choose either the helium-filled balloon or God-box method of finding closure. Either method will work fine.

Once you have finished, remind yourself that the issue is gone. You have been forgiven and life can begin anew. Let it go! You will never live with joy until you do!

Exercises

1. Do you have feelings of anger or guilt toward the person whose loss you are grieving?
2. Which method of dealing with these feelings will you choose? Give yourself a deadline for completing the task of dealing with your emotions of anger or guilt.
3. Continue to think, write, talk, and cry.

Chapter 20
Justifiable Anger

Every loss is unique, and no loss is easy. Perhaps the most difficult losses occur when someone could be held responsible for the death of a loved one. Some examples of this are murder, manslaughter, malpractice, neglect, suicide, and acts of war or terrorism. Often anger accompanies the loss, making grief all the more complicated.

Losses like the ones I've just listed often involve more complicated mourning and may take longer to grieve. A large part of the complication comes from anger directed at the individuals you believe or know to be responsible for the death of your loved one. Such justifiable anger makes the work of grief all the more difficult.

Before I continue, allow me to state that I have never experienced a close loss of this nature. While I have certainly known people who have died by one of the aforementioned means, I have not lost anyone close to me in this manner. Therefore, I cannot speak to these losses from firsthand experience. I have certainly counseled many people who have had losses of this nature, but that is a far cry from having gone through the experience personally. My only experience of this sort has come in the form of non-death-related personal losses that were caused by someone other than myself. As a result of these losses, I felt intense, justifiable anger toward the responsible party (or parties). But again, these losses were of a slightly different nature and not a loss of a loved one to death.

This revelation is made in the interest of full disclosure. Any suggestions I may make here will be things I have learned either from those who have personal experience with this kind of loss or from my experience as a counselor.

Justifiable Anger

Research and study in this area shed light on the subject, and I have also learned a few things of value in my own experiences of justifiable anger.

I have discovered that in the long run, anger, whether justified or not, hurt me more than it hurt the person with whom I was angry. In the short run, this discovery is of little help. It is only of value later in the process of grief. But early on, I find this to be of little value.

Early in the process of grief, my anger, especially when justified, lets me know that things are not right. It reminds me that an injustice has occurred. This is actually quite helpful in the beginning of the process. *While it brings small comfort, it at least reminds me that something of significance is out of balance.* Were it not for the object of my anger, this loss may not have happened. Directing my anger at the person who is responsible can therefore actually be of some value. This helps keep things in perspective.

Managing that anger and finding productive ways to use it in those early stages of grief can be extremely difficult. It can be helpful to seek counseling as a support.

Eventually, anger takes a toll. It becomes too heavy to carry and therefore stands as an impediment to the healing process. In order to grieve effectively, the anger must be dealt with.

How do you deal with anger? There is only one way that I have found to be effective. The way to deal with your anger is to forgive. Forgiveness gives you the opportunity to lay the anger aside and refocus your energies on grieving the loss rather than on hating the offender.

Now before you throw this book across the room, allow me to clear up a few misconceptions about forgiveness.

Misconceptions

Let's unravel a few of those misconceptions about forgiveness:

Forgiving is forgetting. While it is entirely possible to decide to forgive, it is virtually impossible to actually forget. Fortunately, it is not necessary to forget in order to forgive. The fact that you may remember a wrong was committed does not mean you haven't actually forgiven that wrong.

Forgiving requires reconciliation. In some instances, forgiveness can and even should result in reconciliation. But some people are not "safe" for relationships. In such cases, you may choose to forgive while maintaining a healthy distance from that person. Often, this may be the absolutely best option.

Forgiveness means that what was done doesn't really matter. This statement is *false*! It does matter! It hurt. It was wrong. It resulted in horrific consequences. It truly does matter! It's a really big deal!

Instead, forgiveness says, "What you did was terrible and had horrific consequences. But I have chosen to forgive you for what you have done."

Forgiveness means the offender should not experience the consequences for the wrong that was done. Clearly, this is not true. You can forgive while expecting that the consequences will still be experienced.

On a television program I hosted, I interviewed a man whose seventeen-year-old son, who was a scholar and an athlete, was killed by a twenty-seven-year-old, repeat-offender drunk driver. The drunk driver was convicted and sentenced to prison.

Eventually, the father forgave the man who killed his son. He visited the young man in prison and helped him find forgiveness from God. The former drunk driver now says he wants to be a pastor when he gets out of jail and points to the father as being not only his best friend but his new "dad"!

I asked the father, "Now that you have forgiven this young man and he has found forgiveness from God and a newfound faith, should they let him out of prison early?"

His response was, "No! I love this young man and have forgiven him completely; however, he killed my son and must pay the consequences for the decisions that led to the loss of my son's life. When he is released from prison, I will help him in every way I can, but he must first experience the consequences for the behavior that took my son's life."

The father's response was healthy. He had forgiven the man who killed his son but still expected that he would suffer the consequences for his unlawful behavior.

The offender "deserves" your forgiveness. In fact, no one actually deserves to be forgiven. But *you* deserve the freedom and joy that come from releasing your anger and resentment toward this person. Moreover, you need to be relieved of the taxing emotional burden your resentment carries so that you can reinvest that energy in your grief and eventual recovery.

Truths of forgiveness

Now that we've examined some of the misconceptions of forgiveness, here are some truths you should consider:

Forgiveness does not always result in feelings of warmth or even love. Feelings are tricky things and should not be the test of genuine forgiveness. Nor should they be the goal of forgiveness. It is important to release resentment, but it may not be necessary to embrace warm feelings for the offender.

Forgiving frees you emotionally. Resentment and anger sap a tremendous amount of emotional energy. The drain on emotional resources is far too great to sustain for very long. Forgiving stops the drain of emotional energy and allows you to reinvest that energy in more positive activities. Forgiveness allows you to take the focus off the offender and place it fully on the loss.

Forgiving makes joy possible, makes it feasible for you to give and receive love, and allows you to hope for a brighter future. None of these things are attainable as long as we hang on to our anger.

How to forgive

Forgiveness is rarely easy; and in cases where the offense has either resulted in or at least contributed to the death of a loved one, forgiveness is extremely difficult. As such, it may be helpful to think of forgiveness as a process that may take weeks, months, or even years to complete.

Here is a four-part framework to assist you in the process of forgiveness. Each of the four steps may take quite some time to complete. I recommend writing answers to each of the questions listed in the framework.

This process has been used by thousands of people who have found it to be helpful—perhaps it will be for you as well.

1. Feel it. Begin by simply asking the questions, What happened and how has it affected my life? Be thorough in your answers. Name the offense, and describe in detail the results, both immediate and long term.

Why start here? If the goal is to forgive, it is important to know exactly what you are forgiving. Feel it and name it. Write it down so that you can see in black and white exactly what you are going to forgive.

2. Own it. The questions for this step are, Who did it and how do I feel about him or her? Now we get personal. We name the offender and name our feelings.

For many, the feelings for the offender may be mixed. We rarely feel only one thing for a person. You may love and hate the offender all at the same time. In this case, it may be helpful to say things such as, "A part of me hates him and never wants to see him again, while another part of me loves him and longs to be reconciled."

Writing these things down helps you to understand the complexity of the offense and the range of emotions you feel, and it makes certain you realize the full range of things you are choosing to forgive. This is a healthy step.

3. Fix it. While this sounds simple, this is where the real work begins. The question we ask here is, What am I going to do about it? Now that you understand what was done, how it affected you, who did it, and how you feel about that person, you are ready for the next step. And the answer to the question is, I choose to forgive this person.

This is not easy. It may require some time to accomplish, but it is important to remember that forgiveness is less a feeling than it is a choice. We can decide to forgive even when we don't feel forgiveness. In fact, when we decide to forgive and persist in acting on that choice, quite often the feelings of forgiveness eventually follow. But first we must decide.

Once you have made the decision, write it down. Write and speak aloud the words *I forgive you*. Every time you feel the resentment returning, remind yourself of your decision and reject the feelings of anger.

4. *Leave it.* The final step involves an important question. The question is, How will I now treat the offender?

If the offender is someone close to you, you may choose to treat that person as though they had never harmed you or the person who died. This is the optimal outcome of forgiveness and by far the most desirable.

There are, however, circumstances where the offender is not safe for a relationship. This is true in cases of abuse, murder, terrorism, or acts of war. You can forgive and release your feelings of anger and resentment without reconciling or ever having warm feelings for the offender. Feelings of warmth are not necessary for forgiveness. It is only necessary to release the bitterness, anger, resentment, and even the desire for revenge. These things are poisonous and will eventually destroy you.

Difficult but important

Forgiveness is almost always difficult. Where the offense has resulted in the death of a loved one, forgiveness represents a monumental task. But if you truly want to heal, it is incumbent upon you to forgive. You won't survive unless you do.

Exercises

1. Do you need to forgive anyone? Write down the person's name, and make a commitment to do the work of forgiveness.
2. Write in your journal or blog about your feelings on the thought of forgiving this person. Be completely honest as you write.
3. When you are ready, enter into the process. Follow the framework for forgiveness with no expectation of exactly how long the process may take. The important thing is that you enter into the process itself.

Chapter 21
Suicide

Among the most difficult deaths to accept is a suicide. Often sudden and unexpected, this death is complicated by so many "what-ifs." Those grieving a suicide typically ask, "What if I had done or said something different?" or "What if I had been more aware or attentive?"

It is common for those mourning a suicide to be angry with the victim. This is especially true if the victim's depression resulted in dysfunctional relationships with the family.

Religious teachings often can make this loss even more difficult to deal with. When suicide is referred to as an unpardonable sin, the loss is made to feel even more permanent and hopeless.

I would like to offer a different view of suicide. This view, I am certain, will not ease your pain, but it may at least simplify it by debunking what I believe to be false teachings about suicide.

Suicide is usually best understood as a symptom of a disease. The disease is long-term depression. Severe depression has many symptoms, not the least of which is the inability to think logically. When rational, critical thought is absent, suicide can seem to the sufferer of depression to be the most reasonable alternative to the pain. It can also appear to the sufferer to be an act of mercy toward their loved ones. This, of course, is illogical. But sufferers of severe depression are unable to see suicide as an illogical choice.

If suicide appears to be the logical, even loving, choice to a sufferer of severe depression, can it truly be sinful? In particular, could it actually be the unpardonable sin since there is no opportunity for repentance?

Tears to Joy

I would say that for people who have lost the ability to think logically, suicide is not sin. It is the natural progression of the disease of severe depression. *Just as cancer, measles, and mumps all have a natural disease progression with identifiable symptoms, so, too, does depression.* One of those symptoms is the loss of rational thought. The natural disease progression would then be suicide. As such, suicide for a sufferer of long-term depression would be no more sinful than the symptoms and progression of any other disease. I cannot see a loving God holding such a person responsible for a disease progression that was beyond his or her control!

As such, I believe it is completely possible for a suicide victim to find salvation and eternal life with Jesus. I do not believe this is a sin, much less an unpardonable sin. It is, instead, a symptom of a devastating disease.

This understanding will not do much to ease the pain of grief, though it may simplify it a bit. It may also open the door to the hope of seeing your loved one again. This hope, I believe, is very real!

Exercises
1. Have you lost someone to suicide? In what ways is this loss more difficult to deal with than other losses?
2. Have religious teachings helped your grief over this loss, or have the things you've been taught actually added to your pain?
3. Do you find the understanding of suicide expressed in this chapter to be helpful? Why, or why not?
4. Don't be afraid to seek competent counseling for this issue.

Chapter 22
Purging and Disloyalty

In recent months, I've spent time going through the boxes Gayle and I moved from place to place during the last forty years. Some of the things I've found in those seldom-opened boxes have brought a smile to my lips, while others brought tears. Memories flood with each new discovery. And amazingly, I've even had a few surprises—pleasant surprises, but surprises nonetheless.

While I'm keeping a few things I've found and am sharing a few more with my family, most of it I'm either donating or throwing away. It's stuff we should have thrown out years ago but were too busy to go through. Some of it was mine, some Gayle's; but most of it was junk.

Believe it or not, there is something therapeutic about going through these things and even about purging much of it. It has become symbolic for me. It is beginning to represent a new start. It's not about forgetting the past or even devaluing it. Memories and love remain with me forever. Instead, it feels like I'm recognizing that while one chapter of my life has closed, another is just about to open. Hope is returning, and its return is being ushered in, to some degree, by reducing the amount of stuff I have.

It may seem silly to some, but there is a real value to this. I'm pushing ahead—moving on—and traveling lighter is helping to facilitate the process.

Disloyalty?

Often when I speak about purging, moving on, or making changes, some people will tell me they feel disloyal when they do these things. I'm not critical of the feeling since I've felt it too. I've come to believe it is a normal part of the grief process.

As we attempt to let go of the past, we often make big changes. Those changes can mean doing things differently than we used to do them when our beloved was alive. It means breaking long-held traditions or getting rid of things our loved one treasured. Even our momentary experiences of joy can feel wrong. Somehow that makes us feel as though we are being unfaithful to our beloved or, at the very least, being disloyal.

Something as simple as removing the wedding band can create a great deal of discomfort. Truthfully, I went online and searched for the appropriate time to wait before removing a wedding band. What I found was that there is no real answer to that question. It's the right time when it's the right time for *you*! But it still feels strange to take an action that symbolizes yet another ending for the relationship.

This is particularly true when a widowed person considers the possibility of dating or even remarrying. We've spent a good many years eschewing any other sort of romantic involvement, and now any attempt to reengage in the process feels almost like cheating.

Again, we ask, Has it been long enough? Am I moving too quickly? Does this appear to be disloyal to the person I've loved for so many years? And once again, there is no single answer to the question.

Changes are inevitable. In fact, the biggest changes have already occurred without your permission or any decision on your part. Your loved one has died, and that has forever altered the relationship. It now exists only in your memories and in your heart, whereas before it used to exist in face-to-face communication, touch, embrace, joint decision-making, and more. All those things are now gone and irretrievable this side of heaven. Now everything else is not so much a decision to change as it is to simply adapt.

The time line for adjustment will vary with every person, so it is impossible to say it's too early to take the ring off, too early to get rid of your loved one's clothes, or too early to sell the house. Relationship decisions are much the same, with the only requirement being that the decision to reinvest in a relationship occurs only after the major emotions of the loss have been processed. If a new relationship is simply a means of masking the pain, then you and your new love interest will pay for that decision at some point down the line.

If you are being honest in your attempt to process every emotion, engage in the activities of grief, and move toward accomplishing goals, then it is

Purging and Disloyalty

unlikely that you are truly being disloyal in any sense of the word. Perhaps it would be good for all of us to worry less about being disloyal and to focus more of our energies on doing the incredibly hard work of grieving.

Exercises
1. Have you been able to go through items that belonged to your loved one? Are you able to purge anything yet, or are you holding on to things?
2. Have any of the changes you've made since the death of your loved one caused you to feel disloyal? If so, how are you dealing with these feelings?

Chapter 23
Of Shrines and Hearts

When I worked as a hospice chaplain, I also did the bereavement support for families after their loss. One of the things we warned against was something called "shrine building."

Shrine building does not refer to the little shrines you may see along the side of a highway where someone died in an automobile accident. The shrine building we warned against was the practice of declaring objects, places, or traditions to be so sacred that no one dared touch them or change them for months or even years on end. To declare that no one may enter or touch the room of a child who died, that no one may go through the clothes of a spouse who passed away, that no one is allowed to use the car of the deceased, or that no one may change an outmoded tradition loved by the deceased is shrine building, and it can be extremely unhealthy.

Shrine building prevents life from moving ahead. *It effectively blocks the grieving process for everyone involved.* It declares that life must forever freeze where it was when the loved one died. No one is allowed to change or move on because the loss is so great that everyone must live in a perpetual state of grief.

This doesn't just happen with things, places, or traditions; it also happens with lives. I've seen people refuse to sell houses, change jobs, or enter in to new relationships—all supposedly out of respect for the deceased. In so doing, they have effectively made shrines of their very lives! Their lives are now effectively restricted by loyalty to the deceased. They remain frozen in time, suspended in grief.

Perhaps a better way is to pay tribute to the deceased by actually living

Of Shrines and Hearts

again! Why would that be better? It's better because it changes the focus to the heart of your loved one.

It's always a good idea to listen to the hearts of people you love. As a marriage counselor, I tell people to listen to more than just the words your spouse says to you. Listen more deeply, more intently, to your spouse's heart. What are the things that truly matter to your spouse? What does he or she really value? Can you identify your spouse's deepest longing, the heart's desire?

Now let's turn that deep listening to the heart of the dear person you've lost. What would his or her true heart's desire be for your life?

I would argue that the person you loved would long for you to continue to live a useful life that blesses others, honors God, and makes you happy. Admittedly, this "moving on" is unlikely to begin for some time. In most cases, a year is the minimum time required to adequately grieve your loss before reinvesting in a radically new life. But when adequate time has been allowed and the heavy work of grief is more or less behind you, it may be time to refocus your attention on truly living again. And in so doing, you will be engaging in a life that is faithful to the true heart's desire of your lost loved one.

Before Gayle died, she gave me some advice. She told me to have no regrets about our life together. While it was certainly not without its failures, it was a great life! Any wrong that either of us may have done, the other had long since forgiven and forgotten. So I was to have no regrets.

But she also told me to "live our life." That meant I was to keep the focus the same. It had worked for forty years and would continue to serve me well in the years to come. The focus for our life together was threefold: faith, family, and ministry. *She wanted me to continue to love Jesus like crazy, continue to remain close to and love our family, and continue to live a life of ministry and service to others.* I have thus far endeavored to be faithful to Gayle's heart longing for my life.

Yet to "live our life" does *not* mean that I am forever to continue doing things exactly as I have in the past. Certainly, my relationships with Jesus and family will change and grow through the years. The family may entertain new ways of relating to each other, new ways of celebrating our lives, and new ways of living. That is still in keeping with the major focus. And I may or may not continue to minister through Faith For Today. As God leads and my needs and desires change, the context of my ministry may yet shift. To refuse to change anything out of loyalty to Gayle is to build a shrine with my life and to fail to hear her heart's desire.

Tears to Joy

I may sell my house, change jobs, remarry, or make any of a thousand changes to my life while still paying tribute to Gayle by living a life of faith, family, and ministry. To refuse to entertain any new possibility may be unhealthy. It may constitute shrine building.

I'm not going to build a shrine with my life or in any other way. I will continue to grieve to some degree for the rest of my life. Memories will remain with me as long as I have clarity of thought. But I pledge to pay tribute to Gayle by truly living again. I will honor her heart's desire by a life of usefulness, joy, and love.

Exercises

1. Have you created any "shrines"? Do you see these as healthy or unhealthy?
2. Do you have regrets about your relationship with the deceased? If so, how do you plan to work through them?

Chapter 24
The Journey, Memories, and Progress

As we approached the one-year anniversary of Gayle's death, I found myself looking back. I remembered the sickening feeling that came to me when we realized her diagnosis was terminal. While there was no panic, imagining life without her was impossible. We had been a team in every sense of the word, living our lives intricately intertwined in ways some couples will never fully understand. Our love was strong, our trust complete, our focus sharp, and our purpose clear. We were, at least in our view, about as "one flesh" as any marriage I have ever witnessed. The measure of my loss was incalculable.

The pain of the immediate loss was absolutely overwhelming. *It was truly all I could do to just put one foot in front of the other.* I cried every morning and again every evening, was depressingly sad throughout the day, and wept openly with every new experience. Talking about Gayle was both comfort and challenge. I needed to talk and tell the stories, yet talking made me cry all the more. Every day my first and last thoughts were of Gayle. Her memory dominated every waking hour.

Everything felt awkward. Family gatherings, church, ministry, social gatherings, cleaning house, cooking, eating, travel, hotels, shooting television shows, holidays, and every day in between were excruciatingly uncomfortable. Life was empty; ministry, almost impossible; sleep, nonexistent; and hope had evaporated. All was blackness.

It was then that I decided I had to take active measures. It seemed like an impossible task, but I knew I would never survive unless I did something drastic. So instead of running from pain, I sought it out. Earlier I described it as leaning into the pain. I introduced activities, contacts, and initiatives that I knew would cause pain. I did them earlier than I would have needed to and tackled them in bunches. I preached at camp meetings, conducted funerals, taught a marriage seminar, traveled for pleasure (interesting word for it), went back into the studio, and more. The pain was unbelievable, but afterward I knew I had accomplished something. Writing about these experiences, my memories, and my feelings also began to help. Keeping an exercise regimen combined with regular prayer also had a positive effect.

About five months after the loss, I began to feel noticeable improvements. At six months, I had a bit of a relapse, but improvements resumed shortly thereafter. The holidays were awful, but keeping to the plan of leaning into the pain paid off again. Nine months after Gayle's death I knew there was hope for a future. I knew that, somehow, I would survive and perhaps even thrive. *While life would never be the same, joy could once again be mine. There were still good days and bad days and still times of deep sorrow and tears, but I felt there was definite progress.*

As I approached the one-year anniversary, I felt closer to normal. I could think rationally and was intentionally doing things that signified to me a new beginning. The things I continued to do sent a message to myself that life is not over and a new start is a real possibility.

I'm not fooling myself. I know my grief has not ended and to some degree never will. I know April 10—the anniversary of her death—will not be a happy day, and I know I will continue to miss Gayle in significant ways for years to come. But I also now know that I can truly live my life through whatever time I have left. It is my intention to make every use of the time afforded me. Gayle would not want me to waste my life. God demands that the gift afforded me should not be thrown away.

While the journey is not complete, I believe the progress is real. The memories remain for a lifetime, but the pain has diminished. I praise God for that.

" 'O death, where is your victory? O death, where is your sting?' The sting of death is sin, and the power of sin is the law; but thanks be to God, who gives us the victory through our Lord Jesus Christ" (1 Corinthians 15:55–57, NASB).

The Journey, Memories, and Progress

Exercises
1. Are you seeing any progress in your journey of grief? If so, what things make you feel as though progress is being made?
2. It may be helpful at some point to write a summary of your journey through grief. What were those first few days after the loss like for you? How did things change as the weeks passed? Where are you now in that journey?

Chapter 25

Severe Mercies, Amazing Grace

Pancreatic cancer can be an extremely painful cancer. Some who read this will testify as to just how terribly their loved ones have suffered from the disease. Gayle's pain was managed with Tylenol and Advil right up until she went into a coma. This was a real mercy for her but a severe mercy.

It is my understanding that certain cancers can create a condition known to laypeople as simply "sticky blood." This can result in blood clots forming in the body. In Gayle's case, as clots broke off, they went to her brain, causing strokes. The strokes took her eyesight, reduced the sensations in her hands, and more. But as terrible as the strokes were, they were also far less painful than pancreatic cancer tends to be. The strokes took Gayle's life, sparing her from much of the pain of cancer. This was a mercy but a severe mercy.

And yet in the midst of this, we also saw amazing grace. I saw God's grace in the cards and letters we received from friends, family, and people we didn't know at all! Many told of how they had been touched by Gayle's ministry on television, while others spoke of her ministry in the classroom or church, but all had experienced God's grace through her ministry. Children in classrooms across the country sent cards, letters, drawings, and more as an expression of their love and support. They prayed for Gayle, hoping for a miracle. Literally thousands sent messages of tender concern on Facebook and via email. Their lives had been in some way enriched by Gayle, and so they prayed and gave their expressions of love.

Couples contacted us, telling us that their marriages had been saved or enhanced by Gayle's ministry. Women communicated with us, stating that even though they had never actually met Gayle, her life had inspired them to be women of dignity and grace.

As people closer to us watched how Gayle faced her imminent demise with dignity and courage, their faith was strengthened. Even though it appeared that Gayle would not get her miracle, her faith never wavered, and her love for the Master never failed. Gayle's steadfast trust in God inspired everyone who witnessed her last days.

Gayle did not get the miracle we asked for, but by God's grace she was able to *be* a miracle to many who watched her. Her courage and faith inspired many to a deeper relationship with Jesus.

Through strokes, God spared Gayle from the most severe pain of her cancer. But even in the midst of the tragedy of Gayle's final days of life and eventual death, we saw God's amazing grace. I heard it in Gayle's prayers, her tenderness with every visitor, and her steadfast faith. It was evident in her love for her friends, her family, and for me. I saw it in the communications received from thousands of people across the globe. I continue to see it in the stories that are shared with me weekly as I travel and speak. God's mercy was severe, but His grace is amazing nonetheless.

Exercises

1. Where have you seen God's grace in your experience?
2. Have you also seen "severe mercy"?
3. Can you see how the life or even the death of the person you love has also served as a demonstration of God's great love, mercy, and grace?

Chapter 26
The One-Year Anniversary

Anniversaries are incredibly painful. There is no way around it. Anniversaries of first symptoms, diagnosis, death, birthdays, weddings, and more are absolutely the pits!

On the first anniversary of Gayle's death, I penned a blog that was therapeutic for me. It was a brief review of our life together—a retelling of our story. I offer it as an example of how you might choose to deal with or commemorate anniversaries in your journey of grief.

> One year ago today, April 10, 2016, Gayle Tucker passed away. Gayle had slipped into a coma a couple of days earlier, and passed away quietly with one sister, both daughters, and her husband by her side. It was, by far, the worst day of my life.
>
> Gayle and I met while we were in college. We didn't begin to date until eight months after I graduated. I graduated in the spring of 1974. We began to date in January of 1975 and were married December 28, 1975. Once I found her I didn't waste any time. It was early in the relationship when I realized that Gayle was the girl for me.
>
> Our ministry together started early. While it took a while for us to learn how to work together, once we figured it out we never looked back. Working with Gayle became second nature. We not only shared the same ministry philosophy, we also anticipated each other's every move. When we were working as a team we were at our best.
>
> Just this weekend while I was preaching at a camp meeting, a man

The One-Year Anniversary

who is about my age asked to speak with me. He said, "I watched your show (Lifestyle Magazine), but I didn't watch it for the celebrities. I watched it to see how you and Gayle worked together and how you interact. Your love and respect for each other was obvious. You seemed to know when Gayle had something to say and you would draw back and listen as she spoke, and then you would talk. It was done so well! And then the camera would go to the guest and I'd say, 'Get back to Mike and Gayle!' Watching the two of you makes me hope that possibly, one day I could have a marriage like that."

Gayle was a natural as a teacher, pastor, counselor, singer, worship leader, choir director, seminar presenter, and television personality. Her talent in these areas seemed to know no limit, and yet she remained humble and spoke often of the tremendous privilege God had given her of working in ministry. She was by far the most gifted pastor I've ever worked with.

But what most people didn't realize was that Gayle would have preferred to never be the focal point. While she was probably the most viewed Adventist woman in the world (our show averaged over 4 million viewers every week), Gayle would have been just as happy to serve anonymously in the background. In fact, her greatest joy came from being a wife, mother and grandmother. She was tremendously gifted in these areas and absolutely loved every moment of her life in these roles.

There was absolutely no pretense with Gayle. The woman you saw on camera or in front of the church was the same woman at home. I lived with her for over 40 years and can tell you I've never met a more sincere or consistent Christian. Her life was congruent with her expressed faith. She truly lived her faith by showing love to everyone she met. She was exceptionally kind to even the most difficult person.

No one loved children or young people more than Gayle. When anyone seemed to "trash" the children or young people in the church, Gayle became a "mamma bear" rushing to their defense. No one got away with trashing "our kids." She became a second mother to hundreds of kids and young adults. In fact, a number of young people referred to us as "Pastor Mom" and "Pastor Dad," names we wore with pride.

Even in the worst times of her suffering, Gayle never lost her faith. She never blamed God for her illness or impending death. She remained grateful for His eternal, fanatical love and His enduring faithfulness to her.

Tears to Joy

When I asked her if she was angry with God she looked incredulous. "Why no! I've had 60 years of immaculate health when some people never get a day. I've had 40 years of a marvelous marriage and exciting ministry when most people never know anything like that . . ." Then she spoke of her children, grandchildren, siblings and family. Then she concluded, "Should I be angry that all of that lasted only 60 years and not 80? That would seem to be very ungrateful to me. So no, I'm not angry with God. I'm grateful."

Gayle has been sorely missed this past year. Many will feel her absence for years to come. I will miss her for the rest of my days. Hers was a truly remarkable life—a life that touched millions—a life that will continue to have reverberations for eternity.

Sleep well my darling. The morning is coming soon!

Exercises

1. How will you commemorate significant anniversaries in your story of loss?
2. What sources of support can you seek as you deal with the anniversaries? What plans can you make to help you deal with the anniversaries in a healthy manner?
3. Continue to think, write, talk, and cry. These are essential for your road to reorganization.

Section 3

Helping Those in Grief

As you progress through your own journey of grief, you may want to find ways to support others who have had a similar loss. This section will provide a few thoughts on how to do the most good.

Chapter 27
Support

I have in my library a book entitled *"Don't Ask for the Dead Man's Golf Clubs."* I smile every time I think of the title, but then I remember that people can really be that insensitive or worse! Some of my fellow mourners have shared amazing stories of the insensitivity or the downright stupidity that comes out of people's mouths. Their stories make mine look rather silly.

Young pastors and chaplains struggle with what to say or do during times of loss. *I've always encouraged them to simply "show up and shut up!"* My counsel is half joke and half truth. If you show up, no one can say you weren't there or didn't care. If you shut up, you can't say anything incredibly stupid!

Truthfully, there is no right thing to say. It is impossible to say anything that will ease the pain or even truly cheer anyone up. Those words don't exist! And the sooner you figure that out and stop trying to say just the right thing, the sooner you will actually begin to truly help.

Incredibly, the vast majority of people have been wonderful during this most difficult journey of my life. They have encouraged me, taken me out to eat, told me beautiful stories about Gayle, listened to me, offered me a Kleenex when I cried, or just simply "showed up" for me when I needed them most. I can never repay them for their loving support.

By far, most of the people on Facebook have been fabulous! Their love, support, encouragement, and wise counsel have had a positive impact on me.

Someone asked me to share the most horrific thing someone did or said. Well, I don't know about horrific, but I will tell you that one of the most troubling things that has happened is just how many people have tried to "hook me up" with another woman and how many women have been fairly open about their willingness to, I suppose you could say, "take me on as their project." One woman on Twitter has been particularly forward. This has been disconcerting to say the least.

So do you want to be of help? First, show up! You don't really have to "shut up," but it's not usually helpful to try to fix the pain or make the grievers feel better. It's not really possible anyway. You may share a short story about their loved one, especially if it is a positive story. Or simply share your love and pain for the bereaved.

Offer to do something practical. You may babysit, clean house, cook a meal, or volunteer to sit and listen as they tell stories. Make yourself available to drive the bereaved to church, doctor's appointments, shopping, or someplace fun. Something practical could possibly be of help. And if your offer is turned down, don't be offended. You may volunteer again at a later date, but don't be hurt if the offer is not accepted.

Send a card, letter, or email. Again, positive stories of the deceased are great! Everyone wants to know that their loved one is missed and that they made a positive impact when alive. Stories help make that happen.

Don't set artificial time lines on those in grief. One year is not enough for everyone. In fact, some may grieve actively for up to three to five years without being pathological with their grief. While there may come a time when someone close to the bereaved may advise a more intentional and aggressive approach to grief, suggestions that something is wrong with mourners if they aren't "OK" after a year are definitely not helpful.

Pray for the family, and let them know you are praying. *Kindness, tenderness, compassion, and empathy are the watchwords.*

At times, it is simply best to ask, "What can I do?" You may need to ask more than once at different times through the weeks and months of grief. Even if you never get an answer, asking lets people know you care.

There is no way I could ever give a complete list, and of course, everyone is different, so my suggestions may not be right for everyone. But finding some way to share your concern and demonstrate your love is always right.

For the most part, people have done that for me. I truly feel loved and accepted by so many from all over the world. The "Twitter lady" is the rare exception, and for that I am thankful.

Support

Exercises
1. What have people done for you that has been of help?
2. What things haven't been helpful?
3. Continue to think, write, talk, and cry.

Chapter 28
Myths in Grief

Few people actually understand grief. This makes recovery from a loss more difficult. In part, it is more arduous because the mourner doesn't know what is normal or what to expect next. But it is also harder because those attempting to help may actually do things that are counterproductive to the grief process. It's not that they are intentionally unhelpful; it's just that they don't really know what to do or say, so often the things they come up with are actually harmful.

In order to help clear up the confusion, here are a few myths about grief.

Myths

Asking what happened and talking about the deceased will increase the pain for the mourner. The bereaved actually need to repeat the story. Talking about the deceased is one of the very best things a person can do when grieving. It can be a tremendous aid to recovery. It also tells the mourner that people have not forgotten the loved one. Most people find this to be very comforting.

It is best for people to grieve alone. While grief does have a tendency to isolate the bereaved, isolation is not healthy. The bereaved need and often want the support of family and friends who will simply listen to the stories without trying to "fix" or rescue.

People can be replaced. Remarrying will not replace a deceased spouse. Having another baby will not replace a child that died. Attempting to make the bereaved feel better by suggesting replacements is not only unrealistic, it can be fairly insulting.

Myths in Grief

The process of grief takes one to three months. Grief can take anywhere from one to five years depending on the intensity and duration of the relationship, the type of death, and the level of support received. The most intense symptoms usually last from six to nine months, with a sharp increase of pain at the anniversary of the death. But in some ways, grief never truly ends. The bereaved will remember, miss, and even mourn the loss for as long as life lasts.

You can reduce pain by offering platitudes. Truthfully, platitudes may increase pain and produce anger. Phrases such as "she's in a better place now," "God needed another flower for His garden," "at least you have another child," "he lived a full life," or "you're young; you can remarry" minimize the loss and increase the pain.

It is unhealthy for those in grief to laugh. The truth is that it is unhealthy for anyone to grieve all the time. It is not disloyal to the deceased to laugh or enjoy life. In fact, it is usually a good sign that progress is being made.

Don't bother those in grief by calling them to see how they are, especially on anniversaries, birthdays, and holidays. You are not bothering them. People in grief feel very alone on those days, and knowing someone is thinking about them is of tremendous help.

People in grief who occasionally think they see or hear the deceased are crazy and need help. Actually, it is quite common for someone to see or hear the deceased, especially among widows and widowers. Some have suggested that this is the subconscious mind longing and searching for the deceased. It is quite normal and does not represent a mental illness.

You never get over the pain of a loss. Most people who believe this were not allowed to grieve. Therefore, the wound was not allowed to heal. To remember without pain is the goal of grief recovery, and it is obtainable. Thus, it is possible to continue to remember or even mourn without the intense pain of grief.

Grieving is a sign of a lack of spirituality. Grief is a fact of human existence. Deeply spiritual people grieve. The apostle Paul lets us know that we grieve, but not as those who have no hope (1 Thessalonians 4:13–18). The Christian hope of the resurrection does not take away the pain of loss; instead, it helps us place our grief in perspective.

Exercises

1. Continue to think, write, talk, and cry.
2. Have you believed any of the myths about grief? If so, which ones?
3. What things have people done in an attempt to help you that actually proved to be counterproductive?

Chapter 29
Vacations From Grief

It is unhealthy for anyone to spend twenty-four hours a day, seven days a week, submerged in the deepest waters of grief. From time to time, it may be healthy to take, as it were, a vacation from grief. As silly as this may seem, it can be a healthy tool to use as you progress. One of the things you can do for others who are in the midst of their journeys is, when the time is right, assisting mourners in taking these vacations.

A vacation from grief can be something as simple as taking a bubble bath, reading a novel, or going to a movie. Or it can be as big as traveling to a vacation spot for a weekend or even a week or two. I played golf from time to time in order to take a vacation from my pain, and I even took a cruise by myself in an effort to have a respite from grief.

When I teach grief-recovery classes, I give the participants an assignment every now and then. I tell them to find a way during the coming week to take a vacation from grief. The vacation may last an hour, or it may last days. But I tell them to find something they can do to give themselves a respite from their pain. One member of the class took me at my word and took an impromptu trip to Las Vegas! Now this isn't something I would normally advise since it is quite possible for someone in grief to make bad decisions regarding alcohol consumption and even problem gambling, but it was a decision that worked pretty well for a woman named Janie.

When I came in to the classroom the next week, I found a letter Janie had written and sent with a friend. Here is the letter:

Vacations From Grief

Dear Mr. Tucker,

Well here is your surprise. I'm not here! I'm out trying to be good to myself as I am taking a vacation from my grief.

My husband and I are in Las Vegas. Some time ago, we had planned on taking a trip because I had to get away from the house and away from work for a while. But my mother's illness and eventual death placed our plans on hold. But when you suggested we take a vacation from grief I said, "Why not?"

So we bought our tickets and reserved our hotel at the last minute and took off. We are having so much fun we decided to stay a while longer but that means I'm missing a session. I am sorry for that since the sessions mean so much to me!

I promise to be back next week but in the meantime, I also promise to not miss you guys! I'm going to have some fun.

See you next week!
Janie

Janie came back the next week with renewed energy for her journey of grief. At first, she felt guilty about spending some time not grieving. But when she realized it was actually a healthy thing to do, she was able to dismiss the guilt and return to the hard work or grieving with renewed vigor.

Not everyone can do what Janie did. Some are so deep in the pain of grief that they couldn't enjoy a getaway trip. Others simply don't have the financial resources to engage in such an extravagance. But perhaps you can take a nap, read a book, watch a movie, take a walk, or play a round of golf. Enjoy a good joke, visit with a friend and refuse to talk about your loss, or watch your favorite television show. *If you can put aside the hard work of grieving for even a few minutes, you may find that you have renewed energy for the journey.*

I have found that reading light devotional material is another way to get my mind off the loss and regain strength for the rigors of grief. No doubt you will find other things you can do to take such a vacation.

Supporting a friend through this journey may be something as simple as helping him or her have a few laughs or a relaxing afternoon. Certainly, there are times when you can listen to the stories and process the person's pain, but don't forget that taking a vacation from the pain can also be quite helpful!

Tears to Joy

Exercises
1. Have you ever thought about taking a vacation from grief? Could something like this be helpful for you?
2. What things might you suggest to a friend in grief? Could you help your friend take a vacation from the pain?

Section 4
Moving On

What happens when grief subsides? What comes next? How do we move on to life's next chapter?

These questions cannot be fully asked or answered until one is ready for the next chapter of life. But when that day comes, the issues must be faced, and the answers found.

Chapter 30

Joy in the Morning

Weeping may endure for a night, but joy comes in the morning.
—Psalm 30:5, NKJV

Eventually grief subsides. When all the adjustments are made and all the goodbyes are said, a day comes when you are able to remember your loved one without pain.

When the death occurred, you paid a great tribute to the person you loved. You grieved his or her loss. You grieved greatly because you loved greatly, and this was, in a sense, your tribute.

While you will always miss the person you love and while in some ways grief never truly ends, a time comes when the memories are sweeter and you begin to wonder what the next phase of your life will be. When that time comes, it will also be time for a new tribute. It will be time to live your life, and in so doing, you pay tribute through a life well lived.

Some aspects of your life before the loss will, no doubt, remain the same, while other facets will definitely change. For the most part, you get to decide which remain and which will change.

While I cannot tell you what your life will look like, I can share a few things I have learned along the way.

In my view, any life worth living is a life that is lived for something bigger than itself. One of the best things about your life before the loss was the joy you found in living with and for the person you loved. It is quite possible that you would have gladly laid down your life for that person. Your loved

Tears to Joy

one was a major source of meaning for your existence.

When that person died, you were faced with finding a new reason for living. *This is why it is so important to reinvest the emotional energy you had invested in that relationship. That reinvestment will define you and help to give you a valid reason for living.*

The best investments are those that are made in God and in people. They are far more lasting than those made in self or in things. In my view, investments in God and in people bring the best chances of a life of value, joy, and purpose. They make your life a thing of beauty.

As for me, I will continue to engage in ministry whether I am paid or do so as a volunteer. Ministry is my service to God. It is my opportunity to invest in the lives of others. Ministry gives me joy.

I will also continue to invest in the lives of my family and friends. I am still a parent and a grandparent. I love my family and would do anything for them. That investment provides a genuine source of purpose for me.

Many who have lost a spouse may choose to remarry, while others feel a new relationship is not for them or simply never find the right person to marry. I have found myself among those who prefer to remarry, having found someone who is anxious to partner with me in ministry. It is my prayer that our union will not only bring joy to both of us but will also enhance the quality of our service to God and ministry to others.

While I cannot tell you how to reinvest, I do recommend God and people as the assets that provide the best return on investment. If you have lost a spouse, you may or may not remarry. That is of less importance than you might think. What is of greater importance is that you choose to live your life for others.

Whatever you choose, it is my prayer that the tears that have inhabited your nights will dissipate so that you may embrace the morning joy.

Exercises

1. While understanding that the details may change in the coming months and years, what reinvestments do you plan to make in your life?
2. What are the great purposes of your life? How will these purposes play themselves out in the details of daily life?
3. You may decide to read back through your journal or blogs. What have you learned from them? Have you noticed any patterns or gained new insights?
4. Find a way to share what you've learned through your grief. Are there people you know who are just beginning a similar journey? Might you be of help to them?